"Todd Zaugg is the real deal. He has the unique ability of REALLY connecting with his audience via his communication style, life experiences and practical steps that participants begin to practice and apply immediately. He has made a dramatic impact to our sales organization by taking us from "knowing" to "doing".

JAMIE PETERSON, DIRECTOR OF SALES, BOSTON SCIENTIFIC

"Todd is a gifted speaker who captivates, motivates and inspires his audience. He communicates with humor, sincerity and an authenticity that is rare among speakers. I have worked with Todd over the past 5 years and find him to be one of the best within our industry. His style and content will motivate and educate an audience in way that will leave a lasting impression."

LARRY FOSTER, SENIOR DIRECTOR, TRANS1

Todd displays a humble confidence born from a depth of experience… (he) has the knowledge, experience and confidence to fully engage the entire room from the opening bell. His unique insights and disarming style pull participants in and the real world utility of his teachings keep them there throughout.

JOHN DAVIS, VP OF SALES, ST. JUDE

I have had the privilege of working with Todd and Matrix Achievement Group for the past 6 years in Europe and in the USA. Todd is able to connect with sales-people and sales managers to a point where he can have them "eating out of his hand"…..It is truly a breath of fresh air to have a trainer that you know will stimulate your sales-force and sales management to a point where you know implementation will happen.

NIGEL HIRCOCK, GLOBAL DIRECTOR OF TRAINING, COVIDIEN EBD

If you have heard Todd speak, you will find he provides the same energy, direct approach and comprehensive explanations in Warrior Sales Monk that he offers in the Sales Training Room or in the Board Room. I highly recommend that Warrior Sales Monk sit on the desk of sales professionals at every level, pages dog eared and coffee stained, but ready and waiting to offer the advice, backed by real world testimonials, to get the deal closed and the sale won.

ERIC TIMKO, CEO, NUEROVASX

Todd has captured the best ideas and techniques used in the sales profession and managed to translate them into easy to apply fundamentals. I have since added many of his logical principles to my sales toolbox.

ERIK O'BORSKY, CEO OF CCS

Todd has great credibility and passion for this topic and book. He demonstrates that he understands sales people by giving the "what," the "why" and the all important "how." It is bite sized, perfect for reading in 10 minute increments.

RENIE MCCLAY, PRESIDENT OF INSPIRED LEARNING LLC, AND EDITOR OF FORTIFY YOUR SALES FORCE

WARRIOR
SALES
MONK

WARRIOR SALES MONK

Heart of a warrior

Soul of a monk

Mind of a professional

TODD ZAUGG

Published by Advantage, Charleston, South Carolina.
Member of Advantage Media Group.

ADVANTAGE is a registered trademark and the Advantage colophon is a trademark of Advantage Media Group, Inc.

Printed in the United States of America.

ISBN: 978-1-59932-152-3
LCCN: 2009938835

This publication is designed to provide accurate and authoritative information in regard to the subject matter covered. It is sold with the understanding that the publisher is not engaged in rendering legal, accounting, or other professional services. If legal advice or other expert assistance is required, the services of a competent professional person should be sought.

Additional illuminations are available in hardcopy, online or for bulk purchase for sales promotions, premiums, and fundraising. Special versions or book excerpts can also be created to fit specific needs. For more information, please contact www.warriorsalesmonk.com.

For more Advantage Media Group titles, please visit us online at advantagefamily.com

CONVENIENT PERSONALIZED PERFORMANCE SOLUTIONS

WHY IS THIS BOOK DIFFERENT?

- It connects philosophy with tactics. Which increases performance because it delivers not just the "how" but the "why". This book will move you from understanding the philosophical and attitudinal perspectives to real-world tools and insights to help make you more successful.

- It is written the way that salespeople think and learn. Unlike most sales books   that read like a novel, this book has short messages with action plans.

- It is a collection of best practices from more than 11,000 salespeople.

- **Proven** (based on research and real-world personal experiences of successful salespeople)

- **Practical** (easy to understand and use; like a compass, they point you in the right direction)

- **Powerful** (when used, they yield tangible results)

- **Know Thyself:** the most difficult thing to accomplish in this human experience called life.

- Road Map for increased performance.

- Connects your soul to your work/life in order to create sustainable performance.

DEDICATION

I would like to dedicate this book to all sales executives. Your job is lonely, misunderstood, and critical to the lifeblood of any organization. Thank you for putting yourself on the line every day to push your organizations to stretch and to help the world economy grow (like a pebble thrown into a pond ... the ripple effect does exist). Your efforts decide the fate of many people, and it takes a special person to humbly accept that challenge and execute that role as an ethical and talented servant. Always remember, your job really consists of these three main things: hit your number, hire the right people, and then develop those people.

I would also like to dedicate this book to my parents, Art and Barb Zaugg. Thank you not only for instructing me on, but also modeling, the behaviors needed to have a great life. Your unspoken impact is riddled throughout all of my good actions. The less-than-good actions I blame on your other sons.

And, most important, I dedicate this book to my wife and children. Callie, your tireless support is bewildering and majestic. Thank you for your patience and understanding during this journey. You are gorgeous, bright, and the ultimate sounding board. To my children: Chancellor, Peyton and Rainey. This book took years to write and complete. Your smiles gave me the energy to finish it.

THANK YOU

This book is a collection of the "gifts" given to me by family, friends, peers, former managers and other "students" of the sales profession. All of these people have been the catalyst and the content for creating this book. If I have met you, I have learned something from you (including participants of our programs).

To all of my European participants with whom I have worked over the past six years: You have given me many gifts, hours of stories, and a deeper understanding that we are all connected.

Individuals who have had a specific impact on this book (and many cases were my sounding boards):

Charlie Johnson: a true master teacher and guru. He understands the intersection of education and performance. He has one of the biggest hearts on the planet. He patiently guides you and supports you. His company, META (www.metallc.com), has helped thousands of salespeople navigate the dynamic selling environment.

Janice Coggins, Mike Armstrong, Jamie Peterson, Brad Zaugg, Derek Zaugg, Ed Traurig, John Chancellor, John Williams, Jim Heath, Eric Timko, Carl O'Connell, Ken Woody, Eric O'Borsky, Heather Schwartz, Tim Smith.

A special recognition to the ladies who helped with my early editing efforts: Renie McClay, Victoria Andsha, LouAnn Swedberg.

The Advantage Media Group family for their production and support. George Stevens is a talented designer that translates an author's gibberish into tangible art.

TABLE OF CONTENTS

DO NOT READ THIS BOOK

If you try to read this book, it will frustrate you, because not every Illumination is meaningful to you. And, each Illumination is designed to stand alone; therefore there are some that carry over on certain concepts and you will feel as if I am being redundant.

You may consider taking the Sales Obstacle Assessment (online at www.warriorsalesmonk.com) and uncover the challenges that are hindering your sales performance. Once you uncover those challenges, the assessment points you in the direction of what illuminations you may wish to read. Or, You may wish to use this book as a resource by reviewing the table of contents and picking those Illuminations that speak to you and your current challenges.

Utilize this book in the following manner:

- **Encyclopedia or reference guide** for the challenges that afflict most of us in the sales nation.

- **Motivational quotes** to help you stay motivated

PREFACE

I love salespeople because they put themselves on the line EVERY DAY! They push into the fabric of life and face the risk of failure in order to have the opportunity to create a better life for themselves and those around them. There is no other career on this earth that allows people to change their socioeconomic situation faster than sales.

At a very young age, I became a student of human behavior and persuasive communication. I was fascinated by people who could influence other human beings and move them into action or at least get them to agree to a different point of view. I paid very close attention to their style of delivery, the words they chose, and their ability to connect with other human beings.

My father was a computer salesman. He is a quiet, patient, analytical man whose success completely shatters the concept of gregarious salesmanship. He used to bring home sales-training manuals, motivational tapes, and war stories (and I lapped it all up like a puppy drinking water on a hot summer day). Today, as I watch the top 10% of salespeople across multiple clients and industries accept awards at their national sales meetings, it's evident that these winners also are not stereotypical. They are not flashy, arrogant and super-egocentric. They have a calmness that comes from the peace of connecting their daily activities to a higher purpose, almost likened to a capitalistic humanitarian.

The challenges associated with the landscape of selling have changed dramatically over the past few decades. Those of you in sales roles are calling on the most highly educated and sophisticated customers in the history of your profession. Research shows that consumers and buyers are more informed and critical than ever before.

New competitors are entering the market every day. Outsourcing and global markets are a way of life.

It is in this competitive and complex environment that Matrix is compelled to introduce <u>Warrior Sales Monk</u> as a collection of philosophies, behaviors and tactics to help keep you focused on the things that can make you successful.

Salespeople have to keep their skills sharp in order to maintain a competitive advantage. At my firm, we spend a lot of time helping companies define the key competencies of a salesperson as they relate to marketplace dynamics. Our work is very skills-based in that we focus on honing skills needed for customer-centric selling, developing consultative solutions, navigating negotiations, competitive conversion strategies, and so on. After defining the competencies, we spend time training the sales force (including the sales management team) to achieve new levels of performance.

Through the years, it has become clear that while skills are critical, successful salespeople hold themselves to *philosophical concepts* that provide the strategy, focus and attitude to be a winner. You must have the desire, a higher purpose (your personally defined spiritual connection to the endeavor) in order to be successful. In other words, the philosophical concepts and attitudes you hold are as important as the actual skills that you employ. Sure, you can have short-term success without connecting your activities to a higher purpose (and we've all seen it), but who wants to be a brilliant light that flashes and extinguishes like a falling star?

Too many sales-related books available today have become so technique-based (even from individuals who have never actually sold) that they create a void that screams for attention. I have been a student of this profession all my life. This book provides an outlet for me, a cathartic effect, to express the philosophical and tactical components that we have witnessed to exist in the BEST OF THE BEST sales representatives and leaders across many industries. I hope it brings out the Warrior Sales Monk in each of you as it provides encouragement, professional development and meaningful success.

If you can't explain it simply, you don't understand it well enough.

ALBERT EINSTEIN

INTRODUCTION

SALES: THE OLDEST PROFESSION IN THE WORLD?
Bogus. Absolutely bogus. In fact, unboguselievable.

That's how we feel about anyone saying that SELLING is NOT the oldest profession in the world. Someone who supports that concept is just not paying attention. Nothing has been achieved in the history of mankind, or gets done in today's world, without using persuasive communications skills to influence other human beings. In fact, you show me any successful businessperson (attorney, surgeon, entrepreneur, CPA, government leader) and I'll show you a person who has mastered the art and skill of persuasive communication. In many ways, current careers (surgeon, attorney, entrepreneur, etc.) are merely subcategories of the profession of selling!!!!!!

Think about it. It's absolutely true. We've personally spent enough time with all of those professions to tell you that the great separator, beyond the baseline of competence, is the ability to influence (sell) other human beings. Research has shown that incompetent surgeons who have a great bedside manner are sued less often than competent surgeons who have a terrible bedside manner!!!(*) Perhaps it's time to make persuasive communications skills a <u>professional prerequisite for any career.</u>

Maybe the hang-up is the word "profession." Some people find it hard to believe that selling can qualify as a profession, since many successful salespeople initially fumbled, bumbled or stumbled into sales. More important, the sales profession has a negative connotation because many in the field haven't treated it like a profession and therefore have tainted (through lackluster customer interaction, aggressive behaviors, and unethical behaviors) one of the most satisfying careers in the world. Keep in mind, this happens in all professions.

There are some doctors, attorneys, teachers and CPAs who give their professions a bad name as well.

Perhaps it would be helpful to define "selling" or "sales." A sales manager one told me, "Selling is the art of influencing people to do what is in their best interest." This definition has always provided me with a clear conscience, because it forced me to focus on how my solution truly would help my customer. And, it made me stop thinking of me (hitting quota)!!! The only problem with this definition is it states that selling is an art. In reality selling is a science (specific, repeatable steps) as well as an art (implementation or delivery of those steps).

It's no big deal if you didn't choose sales as a profession (it just "appeared" as an option to produce an income). Now, you find yourself having to sell every day and you are starting to question your desire to be in sales. Let's be honest. That is exactly how many of us found ourselves in sales. The reality is that sales skills will help you be successful the rest of your life no matter what you choose to do going forward.

SALES: PHILOSOPHY, SCIENCE AND ART

Ability is what you're capable of doing. Motivation determines what you do. Attitude determines how well you do it.

LOU HOLTZ

It's a new world. Gone are the days in which salespeople ruthlessly rolled over prospects and customers in pursuit of quota attainment. That model was espoused and failed as prospects and customers got more sophisticated (e.g. they've seen and heard it all). Today, we know the truth is that successful salespeople connect a customized higher purpose to their work and use their value systems as their catalyst for success. Their philosophies and value systems give them clarity to the question "why?" which in turn fuels their drive to succeed today as well as tomorrow. And in return, these value systems unconsciously create a loyal customer.

In <u>Warrior Sales Monk</u>, we've captured the *science* of the core philosophies, attitudes, behaviors and skills of successful salespeople and boiled them down. The *art* will come in the way you individualize and use the science of successful philosophies and sales techniques. Why are we including the philosophies of successful salespeople and not just jumping into the tactics? Because of the following formula:

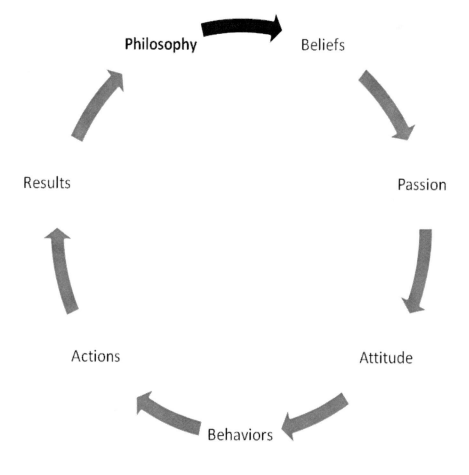

WHAT ARE ILLUMINATIONS?
WHAT ARE "PERFORMANCE PACKS"?

We've categorized the philosophies, behaviors and tactics into Illuminations. The Illuminations are insights, not specific statements of "you have to do it this way." You should process these simple insights within the architecture of your life experience, taking into consideration who you are as a person, the stage of your journey, and the context of your selling environment. The content of this book is meant to be a catalyst – a platform to promote thought and ignite productive action. The intent is that by reading the Illuminations you will:

- "Get your head right" for sustained performance
- Maximize your time
- Increase the propensity of success associated with every sales call

Each Illumination is written in a short and succinct passage. All are based on research or collective experience. It's up to you to connect the dots of the Illumination and your real-life sales situations.

A combination of illuminations, that are related to the same skill development are called "performance packs".

This is a comprehensive collection that is meant to be a catalyst for further thought, discussion and customization.

Many of these Illuminations and performance packs are three-hour workshops or two-day professional development programs.

Connect a higher purpose to your activities and you will have a winning formula for wildly meaningful success.

HOW TO EXPERIENCE THE ILLUMINATIONS

*All that is true, by whomsoever it has been
said, has its origin in the spirit.*

THOMAS AQUINAS

To maximize this manuscript, imagine the following Illuminations to be like a magical mirror that is found in the tower of your subconscious mind. To get the magical mirror to function, you must first reach out and touch the mirror with purposeful and intentional effort and utter the words, "I wish to be enlightened in order to serve." Then truly focus on connecting your energy to the sole purpose of helping your prospects and customers achieve their wants and needs. It is then, when the mirror measures your untainted desire (not your talent, looks or weaknesses) that the richness of the Illumination will be revealed to the Warrior Monk.

*People wish to be settled. Only as far as they
are unsettled is there any hope for them.*

RALPH WALDO EMERSON

WARNING: Do Not use this for the dark side

If you use the following secrets for the dark side (intentionally taking advantage of people), you will be boiled in the stench of a lifeless existence. This existence will eventually drape itself on you like a worn and body-odor-infested coat. The smell will follow you everywhere.

Alas, some people will not recognize this coat when it is hanging on the rack … for the coat will look dazzling and life-changing as it beckons them to make a quick purchase. That short-term and selfish impulse to obtain the coat … that is the same chemical reaction that changes the properties of the coat.

The only ones among you who will be really happy are those who will have sought and found how to serve.

ALBERT SCHWEITZER

Where the spirit does not work with the hand, there is no art.

LEONARDO DaVINCI

Go to www.warriorsalesmonk.com for additional assessments to measure yourself against the philosophies, behaviors and tactics of top performers, as well as to learn more about yourself, and to become wildly successful.

We are constantly adding new illuminations and performance packs on the website in order to create on-demand performance solutions.

1. WARRIOR SALES MONK

Sometimes a mountain, sometimes a valley.

TAO

The heart of a warrior, the soul of a monk, and the mind of a professional…these are the foundations for sales excellence.

TAZ

The will to win, the desire to succeed, the urge to reach your full potential.…..these are the keys that will unlock the door to personal excellence.

CONFUSCIOUS

WHAT? What do we mean by the Warrior Sales Monk? At first glance, the term seems incompatible. Yet, it is clear from our research and the time spent with top-performing salespeople that they exhibit two main dimensions: part Warrior and part Monk. In many ways, this shouldn't surprise us, because history shows us that the baseline DNA of high-performing individuals consists of being committed to a customized higher purpose (a spiritual purpose) and then having the courage to push into environments fraught with the propensity for failure. In fact, most of the revered military forces (Samurai; Knights Templar; Spartans; Swiss Guard; Japanese Warrior Monks; Navy SEALs, etc.) have held a higher purpose that drove their training and shaped their victories. They are warriors in their courageous efforts to do whatever it takes to make their spiritual vision a reality. Selling requires that type of energy and drive. It also requires another dimension: that of the contemplative, spiritually connected (higher purpose), and empathetic servant. This is the Monk aspect. We have seen over and over that successful salespeople have both dimensions and are comfortable using each one appropriately (at the right time and in the right environment).

SO WHAT? It has become clear that while skills are critical, successful salespeople hold themselves to philosophical concepts that provide the strategy, focus and attitude to be a winner. You must have the desire and/or a compelling mission in order to be successful. The philosophical concepts and attitudes you hold are equally important to the actual skills that you employ.

While driven, these top-performing salespeople are fierce about being customer-centric. In general, top performers are contemplative, intentional, patient, service-oriented, empathetic, compete against themselves, and they have to believe in the product or solution that they are selling. All of these traits make up the Monk dimension of successful salespeople.

At the same time, top-performing salespeople are courageous, emotionally resilient, impatient, mentally tough, compete against others, risk-takers, blunt, and short-term-goal oriented (6-18 months of mentally scripted activities that drive goals) with long-term general goals. All of these traits are best described by using the term Warrior for this dimension of successful salespeople.

The magnification and leveraging of your Warrior or Monk dimension depends upon the context of your sales environment: your customer; your products (commodity? technical?). Some people are more Monkish and some people are more Warriorish. Their success is determined by matching their degree of these dimensions to the right selling environment (How many times have we seen top sales reps leave their industry and fail in another industry? Did they lose their skills or did they continue to use their dimensions and those dimension degrees were not a good fit?) as well as matching the right dimension to the customer's personality (Does the customer want a Warrior or Monk?).

THE REAL WORLD I recently attended a national sales meeting for a client in which a perennial top performer gave a quick talk about the best practices for driving sales. Her name was Pam Gord. She is a mother of six and is one of the most passionate salespeople that you will ever meet. (How else can you be a mother to six children and be a consistent top performer?) She was selling products and solutions that were designed to make sure that health-care workers and patients did not get injured during patient transportation. She was explaining to the group of salespeople how she communicates and emotionally engages her buyers. And to explain, she showed them (by having audience members participate) what she does. She said, "could 10 of you please stand up? Now, of the 10 standing, six of you will get back injuries from lifting the patient (please sit down), two of you will get knee problems (now please sit down) ... the two of you left standing are feeling pretty good. However, in the real world you really don't know which of you will be left standing!!" It was such an interactive and emotionally engaging presentation that I now call it "the stand up statistic"!!!! She went on to say that she tells all of her buyers, "I understand that you may not be buying from me today, but I want you to know that I believe in my product so much that I am going to be pleasantly persistent until I can finally help you and help your patients." That takes courage ... and being a passionate empathetic servant ... to pull that off. She truly epitomizes a balanced Warrior SALES Monk.

Many times, it is not just what you say but how you say it!!! Eighty percent of human communication (body language, intonations, etc.) is not done via words. I've seen people ask the same question and get totally different responses from the customer (a sales rep asked the question in the first meeting and then the VP of sales asked the question in a later meeting) because of how the question was delivered. The VP was too aggressive (too much a Warrior) while the rep's delivery was more Monkish, and ultimately the customer wanted to work with the Monk (rep) but didn't like the Warrior (VP).

NOW WHAT? Review the different traits that make up the Monk or Warrior dimension (see the chart below).Where are you on the Monk/Warrior scale? Take the full self-assessment (www.warriorsalesmonk.com) or review and circle the words below that you feel are representative of your nature. Ask yourself which traits need to be leveraged more and which traits need to be "managed" more for your current sales environment .

WARRIOR	MONK
• Courageous	• Contemplative
• Assertive	• Service-oriented
• Structured	• Empathetic
• Driven	• Counselor
• Self-reliant	• Relaxed
• Efficient	• Even-tempered
• Conservative	• Accommodating
• Achievement	• Higher purpose
• Initiative	• Reflective
• Skillful (works on skills)	• Knowledgeable (collects knowledge)
• Learns for specific "purpose"	• Learns for "fun"
• Impatient	• Patient
• Risk-taker	• Planner
• Goal-oriented	• Collaborator
• Formal	• Sacrifices to maintain relationships
• Focused	• Sensitive
• Leader	• People-oriented
• Action-oriented	• Defines self by connecting with other people (relationships)
• Sacrifices for goal	• Has to believe in the solution/ product being sold
• Defines self by accomplishments	• Holistic self-help
• Candid	• Competes with self
• Hard-working	• Learns by analyzing/visualizing
• Has to believe there is chance for recognition	• Less formal
• Emotional resilience (OK if customer says "no"	• Self-acceptance
• Competes with others	• Charitable
• Learns by doing	• Defender of human dignity
• Determination	• Problem solver

As a general example of how this plays out in the real world, the Monk (contemplation) and Warrior (the drive to achieve) dimensions are used for pre-call planning, the Monk dimension is used for customer interaction, and then the Monk and Warrior traits are used for post-call review. Great salespeople flip in and out of these traits quickly and hold a nice balance of both at all times.

2. YOU ARE THE PRODUCT

Great salespeople can sell anything to anyone at anytime.

TAZ

All grand thoughts come from the heart.

MARQUIS DE VAUVENARGUES

*Old work values give way to new ones. But the
ultimate test of American work ethic will come
in how well we work to serve one another.*

JAMES MICHENER

WHAT (is <u>your</u> competitive advantage)? Most MBA schools teach that you have one of three choices: product, your price or you. Which would you choose? The answer is that your greatest competitive advantage is <u>you</u> – your attitude, behaviors and skills.

How do you know deep-down that this is true? It's true because somewhere, right now, someone is selling an inferior product or solution at a higher price. Check it out. It happens every day.

SO WHAT? (The Research) In this era, products from one company to the next are becoming more and more similar. So, differentiating yourself in other areas (such as service and perception of service) is critical!! Research shows that prospects and/or customers always process your communication with them in the following order:

- They consider you
- Your company name (marketplace credibility)
- And then your product

Many salespeople reverse this order, and that can get you into trouble.

The American Sociological Association said there are two things that answer this question of why people like other people (from the book How to Be a People Magnet by Leil Lowndes):

    a. Positive, optimistic personality. People like being around "up" people.

    b. Self-confidence. Basically, my interpretation of this would be the passion and belief in yourself and your mission.

This research underscores the old adage: People buy from people they like. NO SURPRISE!!!! We've all bought important things from people we like. And, people who sell themselves first get:

- Higher margins
- Longer customer retention
- Greater market penetration

THE REAL WORLD I have personally been involved in corporate decisions in which the purchase was very commodity-oriented and the final decision on the vendor was determined by how well the salesperson got along with our team.

NOW WHAT? Don't sell your product ... sell you. Take care of yourself because you are the product. Would you let a perishable product sit in the trunk of your car for too long? No!!! Well, don't allow yourself to get overheated or burned out!!!! You need to be "best" for yourself so that you feel good about yourself and therefore others will feel good about you. Your belief in yourself and your mission drives passion. Passion is the fuel we need to drive our engines. Here are some ways to take care of yourself.

- Most important, connect your daily activities and buyer interactions to a higher purpose (the following Illuminations will be very specific).

- Focus on the attitude of yes.

- Work on your self-image every day (even the act of striving to be a better person makes you feel better about yourself).

- Give yourself affirmations (review your "atta boy" file).

- Make time for fun (fill up your own tank).

- Give other people compliments (it makes you feel good).

- Do a random act of kindness (it makes you feel good).

- Get a mentor.

- Clean up your car or office (it makes you feel in control).

- Keep pictures of the important people in your life close to you.

- Hang out with successful and positive people (they are comfortable with themselves).

- Ignore negative people (they are insecure, jealous, limited in their thinking, live in fear, or all of the above).

- Try not to make <u>important </u>sales calls when you're in a bad mood. It's true!!!!!!! Fix your mood fast or reschedule the call (if it's a very important call). Some people have adopted the "clap your hands and smile" to shift their energy.

- Keep your energy up (food, healthy snacks, the right beverages, physical activity, sleep).

- Music is a good way to pump yourself up.

- Take time before each sales call to focus on happy thoughts (like a "swing thought" in golf or tennis just before you hit the ball) – these are enjoyable memories of times with family and friends. Capture and replay thoughts of when you were the happiest in your life. Wrap yourself in these thoughts, like a cozy sweater, before you make a sales call.

- Watch motivational movies and read motivational books. Get your head right. In striving to be best for yourself you may wish to read: Napoleon Hill, Dale Carnegie, Tony Robbins, Earl Nightingale, Norman Vincent Peale, <u>Chicken Soup for the Soul</u>.

- Sincerely laugh at yourself. Self-deprecating humor is helpful and makes other people comfortable. Many times, you can start a sales call with this (as long as the topic of self-deprecation doesn't reflect on of how you'll take care of their account).

- Project and visualize that you are going to stay positive in the face of adversity (it's not what people do to you ... <u>it's how you react</u>). (NOTICE: We didn't say you had to be a cheerleader!!)

- Keep in mind that your customer/prospect loves to quietly absorb your energy. Some of them are energy vampires (and that's OK)!!!! They like feeling your energy; so charge up your energy battery. They can have more!!!!!!!!!

- What behaviors have you noticed that don't get you results: Too pushy? Not pleasantly persistent enough? What can you do to change these behaviors on your next sales call?

- Reach out and talk to your peers who are at the same stage in their careers. At a minimum, you'll find that everyone is having similar challenges (and so you're not crazy), and at a maximum, you may find someone who has a solution to those challenges.

- If you are your greatest competitive advantage, what are you doing to work on your skills, behaviors and attitude? This book may be the first step.

- While YOU are YOUR PRODUCT ... you must realize that it is not about you.

- What do you need to specifically consider working on? That leads us to the next insight.........

3. SOULUTION SELLING

We are not human beings on a spiritual journey.
We are spiritual beings on a human journey.

STEPHEN R. COVEY

Catch on fire with enthusiasm and people
will come for miles to see you burn.

JOHN WESLEY

To possess taste, one must have some soul.

MARQUIS DE VAUVENARGUES

Scientifically creating and then engaging your passion
can drive sales because it provides a sense of meaning
for the salesperson from which springs the courage
to be pleasantly persistent and productive.

TAZ

WHAT? What motivates us? The debate has been raging for centuries. By now, most of us have heard of theory X, theory Y and Maslow's hierarchy. Simply put, motivation is short-lived if someone else creates that motivation for us. However, if we create our own motivation, then it provides for long-term success. If external motivation is the fire that causes you to act, then self-defined motivation is pyromania!!!!!!! (In fact, the title of this book was almost <u>Pyromaniac Selling</u>).

The reality is that most of us don't like at least 20% of certain aspects associated with our job (and when we perceive that number to hit 40%, we start looking for a new job). So, how do we stay motivated and passionate about what we're doing? For sustained performance, we have to consciously connect the steps that create meaningful passion. When we do so, that 40% may shrink back down to 20%. We can never get rid of that 20%, but we can dramatically minimize its impact on our psyche by being highly motivated.

Ultimately, we must constantly strive to connect our personal and positive life philosophies to our motivations and interactions in the workplace.

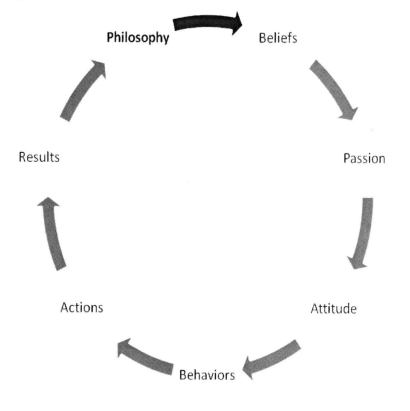

SO WHAT? Tactical passion is your competitive advantage. Simply put, scientifically creating the tactical steps toward passion can drive sales because it provides a sense of meaning for the salesperson and therefore gives him or her the courage to be pleasantly persistent and productive.

And, sustained high performance comes from your ability to connect your spirit (your positive personal life philosophies) to mundane tasks. If you are feeling burned out, you have disconnected from your "real" life philosophies.

For those individuals who doubt that spirituality or higher purpose has a place in business or in the world of economics, it is all around you. In our survey of top-performing sales reps, we uncovered a statistically significant answer to the question "What makes you successful?" Their answer was "I believe in the solution that I'm selling." An example would be, "I'm not just selling a copier, I'm selling the *best* product that will provide the ability for that small business to be more profitable for that owner and employees." We hear statements that are similar to this at sales meetings all the time. (Knowing this information, wouldn't you build high-quality products with the understanding that your salespeople would believe in and sell more of them? Wasn't this the energy behind so many dot-com employees who worked so hard because they wanted to be a part of changing the world?)

NOW WHAT? Today, we present a new model for driving and sustaining sales performance. Scientifically creating and then engaging your passion can drive sales because it provides a sense of meaning for the salesperson from which springs the courage to be pleasantly persistent and productive.

That model is best described as tactical passion and it has two components:

1. Creating the steps of connecting your solution to a higher purpose (something meaningful to you).

2. Applying practical mechanisms that help you to organize your selling behaviors, activities and techniques, so that your passion has direction.

This book will move you from understanding the philosophical and attitudinal perspectives to real-world tools and insights to help make you more successful.

For the purposes of this book, the term "spirituality" is interchangeable with the phrase "higher purpose" and is intended to evoke your personal definition (i.e. my higher purpose is to create a business that employs people and financially helps families; when I attain quota I'll use my commission check to help Habitat for Humanity, etc.). Ultimately, where there is spirit, there is passion.

Salespeople have differing passions that drive them to achieve every day. For some, it's the desire to be number one; some want to truly be a servant to their customers; others desire to create a financially independent lifestyle, and so on.

Many of the following Illuminations will help you tactically connect your spirit to your activities as well as give you new techniques for influencing other human beings (and you may wish to consider the illumination titled **Lightning Rods** and **Lighthouses**, available at www.warriorsalesmonk.com).

Connecting our spirit is critical for aligning the reality of how we influence ourselves and others. Great selling begins with emotional engagement (on our end and the buyer's end) and concludes with emotional commitment (from both you and the buyer). So, as a WSM, we need to constantly be aware that our actions need to follow this path:

Feel. Think. Do. = Spirit. Contemplation. Action

Isn't this the real process that takes us from inertia to movement and action? Any other combination is dangerous to our existence:

Think. Do. Feel. ………………we probably would never "get out of the box" because we wouldn't stay motivated.

Do. Feel. Think. …………..most crimes and bad selling are committed from this point of view.

4. MAN IS NOT CREATED EQUAL

*It is not true that equality is a law of
nature. Nature has no equality.*

MARQUIS DE VAUVENARGUES.

Pain is inevitable. Suffering is optional.

M. KATHLEEN CASEY

*The last of the human freedoms — to choose one's attitude in
any given set of circumstances, to choose one's own way.*

VIKTOR FRANKL

*We either make ourselves happy or miserable.
The amount of work is the same.*

CARLOS CASTANEDA

WHAT? It's true. You're too old to believe in fairies. Life is not fair. Everyone has different abilities, strengths and weaknesses. And, it's a fact of life that everyone is subject to comparison with others.

Here are some examples of the categories of comparison that you and I are judged by every day:

• Intelligence (IQ)	• Emotional intelligence (EQ)
• Expectations	• Fears
• Athletic ability	• Physical limitations
• Capacity to overcome adversity	• Motivation
• Talk tracks (positive or negative)	• Inheritance (allowing access to the best education, additional wealth accumulation, life experiences)
• Our physical looks	

SO WHAT? The comparison list could go on forever. If you get caught up in comparing yourself with others, it can make you a prisoner and paralyze you from achieving quantum leap levels of success.

THE REAL WORLD The truth is that history has shown that people with limitations (as compared with others) can find ways to succeed. Instead of letting comparisons defeat them, they find other ways to be successful. Did you know that 33% of all entrepreneurs are dyslexic? In fact, here are five successful businesspeople who are dyslexic: Charles Schwab; Richard Branson (Virgin Atlantic Airlines); Paul Orfalea (founder of Kinko's); and Ted McGraw (founder of the cellular industry). Did you know that Winston Churchill was a rehabilitated stutter?

The only thing equal among all men cannot be measured physically. It is the opportunity to create the right attitude that will drive them to break the shackles of perceived or real limitations. Everyone has an equal opportunity to create his or her **spirit of attitude**.

Philosophy = attitude = behaviors = actions = results

Wait a minute!!!! **We are equal** in our opportunity to **create the right attitude.**

NOW WHAT?

- Attitude is everything.

- Stop comparing yourself with others. It can make you a prisoner and paralyze you from achieving quantum leap levels of success.

- First be your best and then be first.

- Focus on your gifts.

- Read nonfiction stories that are examples of people who overcame difficult circumstances or limitations.

- Be Forrest Gump!!!! He just focused on being pleasant to other people, on what he enjoyed, and on getting better at what he was doing (without comparing himself or worrying about what other people thought or thought of him). From this point of view, he was a Ping-Pong champion, ran across America, started a company, and got the girl of his dreams. He was oblivious to comparison, and that allowed him to keep his robust attitude.

5.   CREATIVE DESTRUCTION

What got you here, won't keep you here.

TAZ

The only thing constant in life is change.

FRANCOIS DE LA ROCHEFOUCAULD

*New ways of thinking about familiar things can release
new energies and make all manner of things possible.*

CHARLES HANDY

*A live frog that is put into boiling water will jump out of
the water. The same frog that is put into lukewarm water ...
with the water then brought to a boil ... will die, because
it doesn't realize that it is boiling until it is too late.*

FACT OF NATURE

*Even if you're on the right track, you'll
get run over if you just sit there.*

WILL ROGERS

WHAT? The world and the global marketplace are constantly changing. And they are changing at a dramatic rate. In order to remain competitive and not become a dinosaur, you have to be constantly evaluating how to reinvent yourself (i.e. expand your philosophies, strategies, tactics and skills).

SO WHAT? Triumph Motorcycle had 50% market share in the 1950s. Today, it has less than 1%. The business community is full of stories of companies that didn't respond to the changing marketplace (like the frog). Since you are the CEO of your sales franchise, it is important for you to be constantly assessing your knowledge, your skills and your sales messaging (so that it matches what is happening to your customer's industry).

NOW WHAT? Jim Heath, a successful executive of a $6B company, has outlined these principles for constantly re-creating yourself.

- First of all, the very best <u>want</u> to build a sustaining franchise (your sales territory).

- The very best are constantly tweaking/changing their business strategy to ensure their franchise endures through ALL situations.

- The very best reinvent themselves to make sure they are exceeding their customers' expectations and staying ahead of their competitors (this requires becoming knowledgeable about trends that are impacting your customer's business). They review those trends and play "war game" simulations to see how different scenarios may play out and how to take advantage of those scenarios.

- The very best have a three- to five-year plan for a sustaining franchise and constantly refer to it — strategic planning is an ongoing process for them.

- The very best will change their approach to the business, employ new sales methods —financing, contracting, etc., to reinvent themselves.

- This approach allows the very best to deal with market changes, economic downturns, and other sales obstacles.

- While others are relaxing, the very best take their downtime and consider the topics just mentioned.

6. KNOW THYSELF

Real knowledge is to know the extent of one's ignorance.

CONFUCIUS

[Utilize] your every experience — even the most trivial, everyday occurrences — as a means of obtaining that knowledge of yourself that leads to understanding, wisdom, and power.

JAMES ALLEN

There is an objective reality out there, but we view it through the spectacles of our beliefs, attitudes, and values.

DAVID G. MYERS, SOCIAL PSYCHOLOGY

WHAT? Throughout history, from the Oracle of Delphi to Apollo's Temple to St. Francis of Assisi, there has been a common theme … to be successful in life you must first be aware of yourself and the "being" that you are.

SO WHAT? When you know yourself, you can make better decisions, others will be more comfortable with you, and you will reduce the chances of interpersonal conflict. You will avoid over-committing and under-committing to other people and buyers.

THE REAL WORLD my personality could be abrasive to some people because I'm so driven to complete a daily "to do" list. I eventually had to learn to slow down and mirror the personality of other people in order to make them comfortable with me. The results have been outstanding!!!

NOW WHAT? Review the following items:

- Do you have strong self-awareness?

- What is your dominant personality trait (see the Illumination titled "The First Four Minutes – Dead on Arrival")? How does your personality help you to be productive? How can this hurt you in your communications with other people? To determine your dominant personality traits, you can consider the following instruments: the Myers-Briggs assessment; the TIGON assessment (www. warriorsalesmonk.com); the strengths-finders test from Gallup; the Birkman; etc. You should feel comfortable doing this at least once a year.

- Consider engaging with a 360-degree self-assessment instrument (many personal career coaches have these available).

- Do you have a philosophy on life? What is it? Write it down

- Do you know how your brain processes information? Everyone has their own learning and thinking style (i.e. audio learner, visual learner, tactile learner, learn by doing, reading, watching, etc.).

- What are your personal strengths? (Now maximize them.)

- What are your personal weaknesses? (Now minimize them.)

- What are your business strengths? (Now maximize them.)

- What are your business weaknesses? (Now minimize them or work around them.)

- What is your dominant personality trait (see online assessment LIGER), and how does that affect your ability to connect with other people?

- What do you do under stress? Is it a healthy response?

- How do others perceive you?

- What motivates you? Are you motivated more by fear or reward?

- What are your fears? Why do you have these fears? Does it make sense that you have these fears?

- Is there an activity or experience in which you truly love yourself? Do more of that activity!!!

- What do you enjoy doing in your free time?

- Get lost in time. Do you have a hobby or activity in which time flies? Do more of it ... research shows that you are regenerating mental and spiritual energy.

- What productive behaviors need to be reinforced?

- What nonproductive behaviors need to be removed? (It takes 21-23 days.)

- Do you have the ability to "read" other people (understanding the nuances of language and body language)?

- Are you disciplined?

- Forgive yourself: Everyone makes horrible mistakes. Making mistakes is a fact of life. Welcome to the human experience ... now it's time to move on and forgive yourself.

- Embrace failure as a part of every successful journey.

7. BREAK THE LAW: REMOVE THE LABEL

In the vacuum of self-discovery and contemplation,
we allow other people and events to define us.

TAZ

Wikipedia: "Many labels are pre-printed by the
manufacturer. Labels are often difficult to peel and apply.
Some labels have protective overcoats, laminates, or tape
to cover them after the final print is applied. This is
sometimes before application and sometimes after."

WHAT?

La-bel (n.) *anything functioning as a means of identification; especially a small piece of paper or cloth attached to an article to designate its origin, owner, content, use, or destination. (2). A descriptive term; an epithet.*

La-beling (2) *to describe, classify or designate.*

The American Heritage Dictionary,
New College Edition.

It is illegal to remove the manufacturing label from a mattress. Yet, it is critical to your pursuit of happiness that you constantly assess and remove inaccurate labels from YOU. So, break the law as it relates to your personal label ... remove it!!!!

As you read this Illumination, you have a label on every article of clothing that you are wearing. Many of them are difficult to read because that label is hidden from your sight (often on the back of your neck). It would be a lot easier if people came with a manufacturer's label affixed to our bodies. It would contain some interesting information about our content, instructions for use, warranty, etc.

This is a fascinating metaphor, because human performance experts and psychologists focus on the fact that each of us has different strengths. And, some human performance organizations (Gallup) will go so far to say that those strengths were developed at a very young age (~ 4 years old), which harks back to the statement "many labels are pre-printed by the manufacturer."

Yet, for all of us, for most of our life ... our strengths, talents, gifts remain hidden from our view (like the label on the back of our neck). And, because we don't even know that the label, which describes the fabric and the care instructions, is already inherently there for us to review (via self-awareness and observation), we search everywhere else to try to find the "label."

During our search, we sometimes allow other people to define our label. So, we end up with labels that are often given to us by others and therefore not authentic. These labels are based on their experience or perception of us. Unfortunately, many of those labels are harmful, because we let those labels hinder our ability to discover the truth about ourselves. We get so caught up in "accidentally or intentionally manifesting the inaccurate label," or exerting too much energy in trying to defend ourselves from those mislabels (specifically to the individuals who inaccurately labeled us to begin with ... which is the real travesty because those people may have been functioning from the position of jealous, hatred, envy, and never had our best interests at heart). Many of you have experienced the bizarre feeling you get at events (e.g. high school reunions) at which people continue to label us, and you walk away with saying to yourself "they don't even know me." Which is kind of like the singer James Taylor's response to a fan – "I'm glad you love who you think I am" – after the fan screamed, "I love you Jim!"

History is full of examples of labels that have been overcome. Einstein's teacher miscalculated the capacity of her student; society mislabeled Helen Keller; most people mislabel a businessman's failure as "the end" rather than as the beginning; etc.

SO WHAT?

Wikipedia: Labels are often difficult to peel and apply.

Wildly meaningful success is directly related to label identification, construction and utilization.

Individuals who have found meaningful success will tell you that they have found "their purpose" (their talents are being applied to do what they love). They found their label ingredients and are applying them to their life. I seriously contend that you don't need to jump from one career to another in order to find your purpose. Many of us can find a way to make our purpose work within our current work environments (see www.warriorsalesmonk.com for the Illumination titled Lightning Rods and Lighthouses).

The journey of your life is to discover your qualities (your label ingredients), define your purpose, and move toward connecting both of them at the same time. Sometimes you make this connection in your work environment and sometimes you find it in other areas of your life (and if so, it then energizes your work environment).

OK, enough about you, let's talk about that book that you're going to write about how you became successful. One of the biggest impediments to success is related to how we continue to inaccurately label others. How can we know ourselves if we can't even see the positive labels on others? When you start paying attention to other people's positive qualities then you will also start to discover your own.

We label people in our social and business circles on a daily basis for similar reasons. In social and business terms, labels represent a way of differentiating and identifying people that is considered by many to be a form of prejudice and discrimination. Remove the mislabeling of ourselves AND of our buyers.

We assume certain things about potential customers based on what we have been told or by a limited experience we may have had. To assume certain things such as "they always buy from X company and they will never change" is a narrow-minded approach. It limits your potential opportunities. Why do we assume that some people cannot be changed? Is it easier for us to accept our failure to convert? This customer may not be the lowest-hanging fruit on your sales tree, but it is fruit. Remember that the richest and ripest fruit is high in the tree. Let's extend our reach.

If a potential customer is new to you because of a territory change or because you are new to the job, now is the time to wipe the slate clean regarding past labels. I am not saying don't use the information you are given about this customer. Just use it to formulate a series of questions to ask the buyer (in order to validate your information and prior to your solidifying a perception). But, do not create an inaccurate hypothesis because of non-validated labeling. Be especially wary of the thinking that tells you, "They will never buy from me … ." Winners verbally state that situation as "They will eventually buy from me, it may not be today, it may not be next week … but they will buy."

Every VP of sales I know can tell the story of a new salesperson who has turned around a territory that was previously a perennial loser. After peeling the onion back, and after multiple salespeople failed in those territories, the autopsy of success uncovered one main theme: Somebody had finally forgotten to tell the new salesperson that their territory STUNK!!! And, voila, the salesperson didn't know better and hit the quota.

NOW WHAT?

- Break the law … of the pressures of a society and lazy labeling … by removing inaccurate labels from yourself and others. Why? It impacts your happiness and your business. Some people go so far as to find new friends that focus on the positive and accurate labels.

- Pay attention to the times that you feel "connected," joyful, energized (even though you've been working hard). Something about those "moments in time" is communicating the reality of your true label.

- Collect statements of your positive qualities. Look for similar comments about your talents from across various cross sections of people who you know (friends, family, coworkers, managers, etc.).

- Create your manufacturing label. Sit down and write your label ingredients (qualities) as well as your care instructions.

- Stop putting energy into trying to convince other people about who you are … they are not worth your time. Just be authentic to yourself.

- Has your label been an excuse to not try something? Be honest with yourself.

- Labeling buyers. Don't be a hypocrite. Maybe you are guilty of assigning certain labels to potential customers or buyers, and as a result have hindered your ability to build a more meaningful business relationship. Maybe you have accepted failure with certain buyers because of your labeling impression. If so, it is time to reinvent your approach. This will not be easy. It will take analysis and research creativity on your part and maybe on your company's part. But never label a potential buyer as unchangeable. That is just stupid!

- Look at your territory. Determine which potential customers you may be reacting to based on a label. Do not assume that the label cannot be removed. If they are labels you have assigned based on experiences, reinvent your approach. More important, reinvent yourself. It can be the healthiest exercise that you go through as a professional salesperson. The fact that you are reading the <u>WSM</u> shows your desire to get better. Start breaking the law by removing some of the labels that your potential customers have been given. Then, give them a new label – the label of CUSTOMER.

8. BELIEVE IN YOUR SOLUTION

*Most of our so-called reasoning consists in finding
arguments for going on believing as we already do.*

JAMES HARVEY ROBINSON

*A faith is a necessity to a man. Woe to
him who believes in nothing.*

VICTOR HUGO

Man is made by his belief. As he believes, so he is.

THE BHAGAVAD GITA

*Believe it can be done. When you believe something can
be done, really believe, your mind will find the ways to
do it. Believing a solution paves the way to solution.*

DAVID JOSEPH SCHWARTZ_

WHAT? You must believe in what you are selling!

SO WHAT? One of the most remarkable, yet understandable, statements made by the top performers is that they believe in their solution. Wow. This makes a lot of sense (and cents!). Their customers and prospects can sense the confidence and enthusiasm they have for their product. And, the salesperson is plugged in with extra energy to do the little things right.

My first job out of college was in consumer products (Noxzema shaving cream; Raintree; and Cover Girl cosmetics). I had a difficult time really believing in my solution. However, I realized that this thinking was a problem that could impede my success. So I connected the dots and made the following belief statements to myself: These products make people feel good about themselves; and these products help my distributors and retailers make a good living.

NOW WHAT? If you are having trouble believing in your solution or don't feel as strongly as you should, ask yourself the following questions. Your answers will help you connect these dots for believing in your own solution.

- What business problem does my solution solve?
- How does my solution help the main users of my product?
- How does my solution help my customers personally?
- How does what I sell help their business?
- How does my solution help their industry?
- How does what I sell help the world?
- How does what I sell allow me to exhibit my values every day?
- If you have no answers to some of these questions, then you need to continue to peel the onion back. Maybe the conclusion is that, at a minimum, you're helping support the economy. Maybe your conclusion isn't broad enough yet?

9. LIGER: 15 KEY BEHAVIOR COMPETENCIES OF TOP PERFORMERS

*Few things are harder to put up with than
the annoyance of a good example.*

MARK TWAIN

We are what we repeatedly do.

ARISTOTLE (384BC—322BC)

GREEK PHILOSOPHER, PHYSICIAN & SCIENTIST

*How does one become a butterfly? You must want to fly so
much that you are willing to give up being a caterpillar.*

TRINA PAULUS

WHAT? Matrix Achievement Group commissioned behavioral scientists* to review more than 2,000 research papers representing 33 years of research in order to determine common competencies critical to sales success … and the winners are:

- Achievement

- Initiative

- Impact and influence

- Self-confidence

- Self-control

- Interpersonal understanding

- Relationship-building

- Service orientation

- Organizational awareness

- Analytical thinking

- Conceptual thinking

- Information-seeking

- Your dominant personality trait

- Versatility (adjusts to different personalities)

- Hunter (new customer) vs. Farmer (growing business with current customer) focus

SO WHAT? These are sales competencies that have withstood the test of time. If you want to be a sales professional, you need to know where you stand with these competencies. The good news is that if you're below average, most of the competencies can be increased via awareness, knowledge, and a commitment to change behaviors (look for emotional-intelligence training venues or contact us for more information at www.warriorsalesmonk.com).

These competencies are so accurate in predicting success that we developed them into a candidate-interviewing instrument. Our clients use it to benchmark a potential sales candidate against the top performers of the hiring company. The interviewing instrument creates a report that has customized interview questions and suggests a development plan (if the candidate is hired). We named this highly effective tool LIGER (a creature that is both lion and tiger) because it helps find the largest "cats" in the world.

Now what?

- At a minimum, review the above competencies and give yourself a score from 1 (low or no ability) to 10 (extreme ability).

- Have a friend score you on each from 1-10.

- Have a manager score you from 1-10.

- Finally, have a peer score you from 1-10.

You may wish to take the LIGER dimensions insights online. In which case, you can go to www. warriorsalesmonk.com.

> *Fullview Solutions, Inc. (and, specifically, a very talented guy by the name of Paul Bergmann) was commissioned to develop the LIGER report for Matrix Achievement Group, LLC.*

10. EMBRACING YOUR DYSFUNCTION

Do not lose courage in considering your own imperfections.

ST. FRANCIS DE SALES

*Great spirits will always have violent
opposition from mediocre minds.*

ALBERT EINSTEIN

*Normal ... is nothing more than a 'setting'
on the washer and dryer.*

JOHN WILLIAMS

WHAT? Stop beating yourself up about your "quirks." The reality is that there are some dysfunctions that make us productive. Example: Other people are smarter than I am, so I need to outwork them; my parents loved my older sibling more ... but if I achieve, they will love me more.

I worked closely with a world-renowned orthopedic surgeon who started every day at 4:30 a.m. even though he was worth millions. He grew up in a tough Texas household in which his father told him every day that he was not going to amount to anything (he had an older brother whom the father praised all the time). Even though his father has now passed away, this surgeon is still driven to prove his father wrong.

SO WHAT? It is important to understand that quirks can be highly productive. Adam smith (author of Wealth of Nations) was right. The ripple effect of an individual's selfish pursuit "to have meaning" in the world and in the marketplace, is that those people who are so-called afflicted with the need for individual achievement create income opportunities and work for other people. I've seen many successful people with unfilled emotional needs or quirks use their perceived deficiency to generate the energy they needed to complete a project or goal.

NOW WHAT? Use the dysfunction as a catalyst that gets you liftoff toward higher productivity. Then let that engine fall back to earth and rid yourself of that dysfunction forever. Replace it with a more positive motivator.

During my early years of childhood, my family moved quite a bit, and I found it difficult to make friends. I spent a lot of time playing with imaginary friends or creating "play" in my head. I was also chubby (my parents called it husky). This experience gave me the dysfunction of naturally assuming that people wouldn't like me. Since I naturally assumed that people wouldn't like me, it eventually freed me from being concerned about what other people thought ... because I already knew what they thought!!! This background allowed me to pursue experiences that I normally might have shied away from (getting up in front of large groups of people) as well as becoming focused on achieving personal success in order to prove that I am worthy of other people liking me. I also have carried with me high empathy for other people because of my suffering through my perception of the lack of childhood friends as well as the early years of my physical appearance. I've slowly replaced most of that dysfunctional thinking with more holistic motivators, such as helping other people be successful and balancing my life with more enduring time/value opportunities, so that "just" business achievement doesn't define me (family, etc.).

11. EAGLES AND LEMMINGS

*Whenever you find yourself on the side of the
majority, it is time to pause and reflect.*

MARK TWAIN

*Every society honors its live conformists
and its dead troublemakers.*

MIGNON McLAUGHLIN

*I am wondering what would have happened to me if some fluent
talker had converted me to the theory of the eight-hour day and
convinced me that it was not fair to my fellow workers to put
forth my best efforts in my work. I am glad that the eight-hour
day had not been invented when I was a young man. If my life
had been made up of eight-hour days, I don't believe I could
have accomplished a great deal. This country would not amount
to as much as it has if the young men of 50 years ago had been
afraid that they might earn more than they were paid for.*

THOMAS EDISON

WHAT? Do your own independent thinking instead of automatically accepting and following the thinking that is being regurgitated by the rest of the group.

SO WHAT? Your ability to be an independent thinker is a key building block for having a competitive advantage in the world. This attitude drives the behaviors that constantly produce fruit. Look at the economics of this truth. In terms of national wealth, the countries that allow independent thinking have greater wealth at both the governmental and individual levels. Individuals who exhibit independent thinking create new industries that drive personal wealth. Good examples of this include Henry Ford and Bill Gates

In Thomas Friedman's book <u>The Earth Is Flat</u>, he makes the statement that creativity is the United States' greatest advantage in the market. The basic premise is that original thought is an economic force. Many cultures focus so much on book education that they stifle the human brain and soul. Groupthink is counterproductive for breakthrough performance.

A prominent university that has a school of entrepreneurialism concluded that more than 80% of all entrepreneurialism comes from outside the current industry. Is that because all of the people in the same industry attend the same industry meetings? Is it because those same industries hire people from within their industry and therefore continue to perpetuate the status quo? Are they all being hypnotized into groupthink?

On a personal level, independent thinking creates the right atmosphere for working independently. This means you don't need constant direction and you are able to solve more problems, more quickly. The originality of your thinking will separate you from your internal and external competitors.

You don't have to leave your company to be an independent thinker. Intrapreneurialism (also known as "out of the box" thinking) is critical for a corporation's success, and the salespeople who are constantly innovating within their own company build sustainable success.

NOW WHAT? Increase your independent thinking by asking yourself:

- Why am I doing this? Why are we doing it this way?

- Ask a series of "what if?" questions to help come up with some innovative and independent ideas.

- Contact Dennis Stauffer, an innovation guru, for your personal innovation behavioral assessment and training (www.insightfusion.com).

12. Get Out of the Way of Yourself

In speaking of the word "worry" and its Greek etymology, "
... In other words, a person who is anxious suffers from a
divided mind, leaving him or her disquieted and distracted.

Day by Day, Charles Swindoll

We have met the enemy and he is us.

Seneca

We probably wouldn't worry about what people think
of us if we could know how seldom they do.

Olin Miller

They who give have all things; they who withhold have nothing.

Hindu proverb

... I absolve you of worry ... don't waste your energy on "worry."

Brad Saar, president of $500M division of a global
organization, during a speech to his sales force
during the 2009 National Sales Meeting (in response
to a question about market uncertainties)

WHAT? Too many people get too focused on worrying about what other people think of them. By doing this, they actually start building a self-fulfilling prophecy, because their behavior becomes so unnatural that other people do begin to wonder about them.

Consider this. One element of narcissistic behavior is the belief that everyone is concerned about you or your situation or circumstance. The reality is that most people are too busy with their own challenges to worry about you.

SO WHAT? When you focus too much on you and your worries, you get in the way of connecting with other people. Or, more commonly, you think that your customers' response to you is a personal attack. If they get angry, it's more likely that they are having a bad day. Their reaction to you is not about you, it's about other circumstances that are bombarding their lives.

I have seen very talented people ruin a sale, or worse yet, their careers, because they got wrapped up in manifesting personal worries in a way that was counter-productive to business. One example was a salesperson who thought: "Nobody ever listens to my ideas, so during my presentation to the VP of sales I'm going to make sure they know how smart I am. Then they'll agree how good my idea is." I saw this scenario play out. The reality was that no one could focus on the good idea he had because we were all focused on how defensive he was during the presentation.

NOW WHAT? Simple. Get so focused on the following that you forget about yourself:

- Serving your customer
- Making your manager look good
- Meeting the needs of others
- Doing something generous for someone else (like a random act of kindness); you'll find that it actually helps you

13. ARE YOU THE MONKEY?

The only thing we learn from history is that
we learn nothing from history.

HEGEL

The definition of insanity is doing the same thing
over and over but expecting different results.

VARIOUS ATTRIBUTIONS

We first make our habits, then our habits make us.

JOHN DRYDEN

WHAT? Wild monkeys are caught by native hunters who take advantage of the monkeys' behavior of not letting go. The hunters create a small hole in a coconut (just large enough for a monkey's hand) and then put rice inside the coconut. The unsuspecting monkey tries to get the rice out of the coconut but cannot get its hand back out (because the rice in their hand makes their hand too large to remove from the coconut). The animal does not recognize that it could free itself if it would just let go of the rice.

SO WHAT? Are you behaving like a monkey? Are you participating in or clinging to behaviors and actions that are nonproductive? Are there emotions or feelings that you are not letting go that are blocking you from being productive? "Talk tracks" from your childhood may have negatively conditioned you and they may be limiting your ability to create interpersonal relationships and achieve personal and career success.

NOW WHAT?

- Identify those behaviors, feelings and habits that are not good for you or your success.

- Let go of things that are not good for you or for your success. If you're trying to get rid of bad habits, be patient. It takes at least 30 days to break habits.

14. THE FOUR BATTERIES OF PERFORMANCE

I very humbly argue that every major thinker since recorded time has argued this perspective. Christian, Freudian, Confucian, Judaic thinking — all have argued the need for balance between material wealth, community involvement and interpersonal intimacy to achieve success. Without a chronic challenge that ties you to the community, career success is nothing but narcissistic gratification that will doom you to burnout.

STEVEN BERGLAS, PH.D.

If you don't have your health, you don't have anything.

JEWISH PROVERB

Everyone is a house with four rooms, a physical, a mental, an emotional and a spiritual. Most of us tend to live in one room most of the time, but unless we go into every room, every day, even if only to keep it aired, we are not a complete person.

INDIAN PROVERB

Beware the barrenness of a busy life.

SOCRATES

WHAT? Life is a combination of sprints and marathons that can only be sustained by maintaining and recharging your physical, emotional, mental and spiritual batteries.

SO WHAT? Research on human performance shows that there are four key areas to focus on to be healthy: mental, physical, emotional, and spiritual (having a higher purpose). We need time to define and understand these areas, establish goals for each, and then recharge ourselves in each of these areas. (See Illumination titled "Recharge You Competitive Advantage" for more about how to do this.)

It's no surprise that we have moved from the era of self-help (1980s) into physical fitness (1990s) and then into wanting balance in all areas of our lives (2000s). We've been searching for the recipe of complete health for a long time. Until just recently, the journey has been limited in scope since we've focused on only one dimension at a time. Now we know that we need to look at four dimensions that to be healthy.

NOW WHAT? Take care of yourself. Imagine that you have four battery packs for your energy and performance: mental, physical, emotional, and spiritual. Take care of yourself by making a specific plan to focus on each of the four areas. Begin by identifying the current level of "power" in each of your four types of batteries.

Battery Type	Replace	Weak	Good	Excellent
Spritual				
Emotional				
Mental				
Physical				

For those batteries that are weak, consider the following techniques to recharge them.

MENTAL

Research shows that when you try something different (crossword puzzles, Sudoku, reading) it stimulates new neurological synapses in the brain. Or, getting involved in sports requires mental strategy (tennis, golf, etc.).

PHYSICAL

- Eating is a big contributor to the condition of your physical battery. Choose healthy snacks; try eating small meals every two hours to maintain healthy levels of blood sugar; choose the right beverages. (Water helps your skin stay young, keeps your organs working right, and helps to reduce weight, while diet sodas negatively impact your bones.) Consider getting the BarCharts, Inc.® laminated quick reference guide on vitamins and minerals as well as its reference guide on nutrition.

- Get good sleep. Ben Franklin said it all: "Early to bed and early to rise makes a man healthy, wealthy and wise."

- Be sure to exercise. Exercise increases oxygen in the blood, releases tension and stress, strengthens the muscles and body. As with anything, don't overdo the exercise, or do too much too soon. Three days of cardio and two days of strength training are recommended per week.

- Here are the critical vitamins that have been proven to have an impact on your body: a multi-vitamin that is gender specific (men, make sure it includes saw palmetto); omega-3; and restaverol.

EMOTIONAL

- Connect with family and friends on a consistent basis.

- Be sure to get involved in doing something in the community, or just look to do random acts of kindness on a daily basis. Feeling that you've helped someone without expecting anything in return is shown to improve your mood.

- Don't watch, read, or listen to more than 20 minutes of the news – often this can really zap your emotional battery.

ACTIVITY

Here are some common emotional barriers that impede our ability to be more successful in life. Circle the ones that are true for you, then identify how it is impeding your ability to have better relationships.

• Anger/Temper Way it impedes: _____	• Poor Team Player Way it impedes: _____
• Fear/Anxiety Way it impedes: _____	• Poor Listener Way it impedes: _____
• Frustration Way it impedes: _____	• Poor Communicator Way it impedes: _____
• Impatience Way it impedes: _____	• Pessimism/Negativity Way it impedes: _____
• Defensiveness Way it impedes: _____	• Lack of Empathy Way it impedes: _____
• Low Self-Confidence Way it impedes: _____	• Lack of Trust Way it impedes: _____
• Moodiness Way it impedes: _____	• Low Emotional Recovery Period Way it impedes: _____
• Inflexibility on 80% of Issues Way it impedes: _____	• Inflexibility Way it impedes: _____

Now, develop a plan for how you will rewire yourself when these emotional impediments start. For example, with anger as an impediment, count to 20 before responding to the situation.

- **Spiritual** (higher purpose). Spend time contemplating how you view the world and your "reason for being." Come up with a life perspective that you operate from that is larger than yourself. For some, this can have a religious element (and for some people a spiritual experience is giving birth to a company). Connect these thoughts to your day-to-day efforts. Did you know that more than 70% of Vietnam POW survivors said that what kept them alive during years of captivity was their belief in a supreme being? Do you have something strong enough in your spiritual journey that would sustain you in captivity? Read motivational sayings and books. Create a humanistic creed to live by. Here is an example of a creed that I got from a rural Tennessee restaurant owner:

1. Patience is first ... always ... and this
   feeds the "good wolf" of my heart.

2. Never pass up the chance to "keep my mouth closed."

3. Never be afraid to teach.

4. Find a balance between Number 1 and
   Number 2, and avoid large doses of both.

5. My life is connected to all things, especially you and me.

6. I am not in control of all things all the time – fortunately
   – so let things happen ... enjoy the sun rising and setting.

7. No matter what you do, be truthful.

8. Happiness is now. Understanding now is
   happiness, one moment at a time, happiness
   is in the way we act ... not the outcome.

9. Meditate: Breathe deeply ... sit still ... relax ...
   listen ... dream ... repeat. Drink a lot of water.

10. Creation sets you free. Creation of love and loving solutions fulfills your deepest instincts to be good. Your actions are your creations.

11. Learn what you already know. Tell your heart what your mind says. Feed love; starve anger; stop war.

12. Think positively and trust the wisdom and guidance of your heart. You can do it!!!!

And here is one that I created from a similar exercise:

1. Expend so much energy on personal improvement that you have no time to criticize others.

2. Forgive yourself.

3. Forgive others.

4. Perform an anonymous random act of kindness for someone (generous people have mental health).

5. Live simply.

6. Give more.

7. Expect less.

8. Be passionate about something.

9. Be compassionate about everything.

10. Design your life.

11. Tweak your design.

12. Happiness is in the journey of that design … the journey is in every moment.

13. Free your heart from worries and fear … these are the shackles of the devil.

14. You were born as flesh and bone … your reputation is what you create.

If you're a leader of men, you may wish to construct a leadership creed:

1. Maintain the self-confidence and self-esteem of others.
2. Focus on the situation, issue or behavior, not the person.
3. Maintain constructive relationships.
4. Take initiative to make things better.
5. Ethical behavior has an impact on the bottom line.
6. Lead by example.

15. PARANOIA IS YOUR FRIEND

I have been through some terrible things in my life,
and some of them have actually happened.

WILL ROGERS

You're not paranoid if it's really happening

TAZ

Hope for the best, plan for the worst.

TAZ

WHAT? One of the surprising things that we've seen from the best of the best is that they exhibit a sprinkle of paranoia in their character. This is much like putting a dash of salt in a big bowl of soup to add a bit of flavor.

SO WHAT? Top performers stay on top of their game by thinking about:

- What their competition is doing in their accounts
- What they would do if their customer leaves them
- And yes … what their company is going to do to their commissions, territory or promotional opportunities.

Paranoia is productive if it helps spur additional activities that produce business results. Paranoia is a catalyst for allowing the best to "anticipate and then compensate."

A few years ago, I had a funny feeling about one of my accounts. I had been so busy working on new business that I realized that I hadn't talked with this particular account for a while. I had a funny, paranoid feeling that my residual business might be at risk. Some people might have said "Hey, no news is good news," and left it alone. But, I was paranoid enough to pick up the phone and call one of my contacts inside the account. The person didn't return my call for two days, which only increased my paranoia (instead of thinking "maybe they are on vacation"). I called another contact and it turned out that the department was being told by the CEO to "build training materials in-house" and my contacts were feeling sheepish about telling me that my business was at risk. Once I got this news, I built a Ben Franklin decision matrix to show them that they would spend more money hiring full-time employees (a fixed expense) than what they were spending with our consulting firm. Fortunately, my paranoia was well-timed, because the CEO wanted their plan within 10 days. They used my information to persuade the CEO that they shouldn't build out a bigger in-house effort.

Paranoia can be extension of "caring enough" about taking care of your customers and doing a great job in general.

NOW WHAT?

- Understand the difference between healthy paranoia and unhealthy paranoia. Please note that we said paranoia is like a <u>dash</u> of salt in a large bowl of soup.

- Practice the healthy paranoia of anticipating your competitors' response and beat them to the punch (a preventative strike). Now there's the Warrior Sales Monk in action!

16. CYNICISM IS YOUR SHAVING CREAM

When people decide arbitrarily to be optimists,
they may miscalculate when it comes to serious
crises, evildoing, wars, personal conflicts, etc.

DEEPAK CHOPRA, LIFE AFTER DEATH

Rose-colored glasses are a fashion statement, and when worn
can have a negative impact on a financial statement.

TAZ

Facts do not cease to exist because they are ignored.

ALDUS HUXLEY

WHAT? While master salespeople are optimistic, the best reps also have a hint of cynicism. Their cynicism is almost like the leftover aloe film of shaving cream on your skin. Shaving helps remove "stubble" that is blocking a more realistic view of the situation.

SO WHAT? I can always pick out a top performer by the challenging questions that they ask. Cynicism, in small doses, is effective in helping you pretend to be in your customer's shoes. It helps you anticipate your customer's objections and work through potential obstacles.

NOW WHAT? Make sure that you are using cynicism as a way to be productive. For instance: Is it allowing you to consider all the different aspects of your solution/proposal, including the challenges that the customer might see?

Be careful; too much cynicism is not productive.

17. NOT RISKING IS FAILURE

Achieving life is not the equivalent of avoiding death.

AYN RAND

Life is too short to be little.

BENJAMIN DISRAELI

What doesn't kill us makes us stronger.

NIETZSCHE

Twenty years from now you will be more disappointed by the things you didn't do than by the ones that you did do. So, throw off the bowlines. Sail away from the safe harbor. Catch the trade winds in your sails. Explore. Dream. Discover.

MARK TWAIN

Whatever you can do, or dream, you can begin it — boldness has genius, power, and magic in it.

JOHANN WOLFGANG VON GOETHE

It is nothing to die. It is an awful thing never to have lived.

JEAN VALJEAN IN VICTOR HUGO'S LES MISERABLES

He who has conquered doubt and fear, has conquered failure.

JAMES ALLEN, AS A MAN THINKETH

WHAT? Risk is a relative term. It has a scale that is relative to each individual and it is around us all the time. Examples of risk in the sales arena include: territory realignment; a promotion; a new career; a new job; new commission plan; willingness to accept other ideas; willingness to accept others; delegating work to others; starting a new company, etc.

SO WHAT? Fear stops people from taking risks and creating a phenomenal life. Every human being is born with two fears (spatial fear and the fear of loud noises). Any other fear is created by man. Many times fears are self-authored. Every decision has risks, so much so that even not making a decision is a decision that has risks!!!

Calculated risks are acceptable, necessary and inevitable. Most of the great entrepreneurs have been amazed at our amazement of them because almost all of them took some major risks. They respond to our amazement by saying it was a "calculated risk."

How many times have you seen sports teams get ahead in a game and then lose because they got too conservative?

Triumph Motorcycles used to have 50% of the world market. Today, it has only 1%. Not taking a calculated risk in engineering design and marketing led to its massive reduction in market share.

I have a great friend who is a serial entrepreneur (he has faced bankruptcy more than once and is now a multimillionaire). He has his risk scale as such: "Why do I want to be like the other 90% of the working world? The walking robots? Risk schmisk!! Everything is a risk. Being a walking, passionless robot is a risk!"

I got involved in start-up companies because I was convinced that the worst thing that could happen to me was going back into the medical-device world. That final thought pattern broke me free from my emotional response to risk and allowed me to focus on the rational side of risk.

NOW WHAT? What's the worst that could happen to you if you took that risk? Make a list of the top 10 things and then state them out loud. One item on the list should be that you have never taken a risk. Then pretend that you are talking with a friend who just gave you those 10 reasons. What would you say to that friend?

- Fear of failure. Failure is going to happen!!! So what?

- Fear of the unknown. It cuts both ways; what if you don't do it? That is an unknown as well.

- Fear of rejection. Get used to it. Some of the most famous people learned to deal with rejection at an early age.

- Other advice to give your friend should include:

- Are you paralyzed or procrastinating? Are you in a "study too long, study wrong" mode? There may not be any more concrete information that is going to come forth for you to be able to make a decision.

- Get comfortable with possible "event" failures. These short-term setbacks can be great learning grounds for long-term success. Just think: The average entrepreneur fails at least seven times.

- Risk … schmisk. How many times have we seen sport teams get ahead and then blow the lead. By trying to reduce their risk, they actually increased it!!!

18. REALITY MARKERS OF SUCCESS

There must be more to life than having everything.

MAURICE SENDAK

What man actually needs is not a tensionless state, but rather the striving and struggling for some goal worthy of him.

VIKTOR FRANKL

Success is getting what you want; happiness is wanting what you get.

ANONYMOUS

To laugh often and much; to win the respect of intelligent people and the affection of children; to earn the appreciation of honest critics and endure the betrayal of false friends; to appreciate beauty, to find the best in others; to leave the world a little better, whether by a healthy child, a garden patch, or a redeemed social condition; to know even one life has breathed easier because you have lived. This is the meaning of success.

RALPH WALDO EMERSON (ATTRIB.)

To succeed in life, one must have determination and must be prepared to suffer during the process.

*If one isn't prepared to suffer during adversities,
I don't really see how he can be successful.*

GARY PLAYER

WHAT? How can you play this game of life without knowing what a "win" looks like?

SO WHAT? Chasing false realities of success will leave you empty, bummed out and maybe angry. It will adversely impact your performance and add stress to your life. It's critical that you spend time thinking about your definition of success (not someone else's definition).

Another common mistake in life is to measure success by looking at people in the media and using them as a yardstick of success (movie stars, athletes, politicians, CEOs, etc.). The fact is that most of these people are not happy. Their lifestyle and fame have gotten in the way of their ability to construct a personally rewarding life. It's OK to collect examples of productive behaviors, but realize that they are human. (P.S. If you live your life exhibiting the values that you've chosen, you're the one who is famous!)

A study by the University of Rochester's Human Motivation Research Group found that people whose motivation was authentic (self-authored) exhibited more interest, excitement and confidence as well as greater persistence, creativity and performance than a control group of subjects who were motivated largely by external demands and rewards.

Researchers have also determined that there is no correlation between income levels and happiness. Between 1957 and 1990, per-person income in the U.S. doubled, taking into account inflation.

Not only did people's reported levels of happiness fail to increase at all during the same period, but rates of depression grew nearly tenfold. The incidence of divorce, suicide, and alcoholism and drug abuse also rose dramatically.

In 2007, Time Magazine published an article in which psychologists had completed some research on happiness and found that once individuals achieved at least $40,000 in income, their happiness scale only increased by only 1% for every new leap of $40,000 in income.

Happiness makes money but money does not make happiness.

Don't believe that money can't buy <u>some</u> happiness. Most people will tell you that money takes the edge off certain stresses.

MARSHMALLOW STUDY

In this groundbreaking study, researchers took young children (one at a time) and placed a marshmallow in front of them. The researcher then told the child that he or she could have the marshmallow now, or if he or she waited until the researcher got back in 10-15 minutes, the child could have two marshmallows.

Eighty percent of the children ate the marshmallow immediately. Those children were then followed into adult life. The 20% of the children who delayed immediate gratification were much happier as adults. This correlates to today's credit crisis. So many people are in debt because they want everything now.

Everyone experiences stress. Fascinatingly enough, certain stresses are common to our human experience (financial, interpersonal, career, etc.); there isn't a single successful person who hasn't experienced adversity while moving toward his or her definition of success.

And finally, this quick story from the Internet:

MAYONNAISE JAR & TWO BEERS

When things in your life seem almost too much to handle, when 24 hours in a day are not enough, remember the mayonnaise jar and the two beers.

A professor stood before his philosophy class and had some items in front of him.

When the class began, he wordlessly picked up a very large and empty mayonnaise jar and proceeded to fill it with golf balls.

He then asked the students if the jar was full.

They agreed that it was.

The professor then picked up a box of pebbles and poured them into the jar. He shook the jar lightly.

The pebbles rolled into the open areas between the golf balls.

He then asked the students again if the jar was full.

They agreed it was.

The professor next picked up a box of sand and poured it into the jar.

Of course, the sand filled up everything else.

He asked once more if the jar was full.

The students responded with a unanimous "yes."

The professor then produced two beers from under the table and poured the entire contents into the jar, effectively filling the empty space between the sand.

The students laughed.

"Now," said the professor as the laughter subsided, "I want you to recognize that this jar represents your life.

"The golf balls are the important things – your family, your children, your health, your friends and your favorite passions – and if everything else was lost and only they remained, your life would still be full.

"The pebbles are the other things that matter like your job, your house and your car.

"The sand is everything else – the small stuff.

"If you put the sand into the jar first," he continued, "there is no room for the pebbles or the golf balls.

"The same goes for life.

"If you spend all your time and energy on the small stuff, you will never have room for the things that are important to you.

"Pay attention to the things that are critical to your happiness.

"Spend time with your children.

"Spend time with your parents.

"Visit with grandparents.

"Take time to get medical checkups.

"Take your spouse out to dinner.

"Play another 18.

"There will always be time to clean the house and fix the disposal.

"Take care of the golf balls first – the things that really matter.

"Set your priorities.

"The rest is just sand."

One of the students raised her hand and inquired what the beer represented.

The professor smiled and said, "I'm glad you asked.

"The beer just shows you that no matter how full your life may seem, there's always room for a couple of beers with a friend."

Now What?

- Don't set the expectation of having a stress-free life or that you will be happy all the time. Happiness is only one of many human emotions (jealousy, envy, love, hate, anger, joy, happiness, etc.). It's normal to experience different emotions. You will have gray days.

- Take small steps of denying yourself some little things of "immediate gratification" that have been potentially harmful to your health (too many sugar drinks), career, or relationships. Then bask in the feeling of having controlled yourself and your environment. It will make you stronger and give you confidence to deal with bigger challenges.

- You can't be good at everything. No one is good at everything. Focus on your strengths and work around your weaknesses. Unlike other books or philosophies that communicate that you shouldn't think about your weaknesses, this one tells you that the reality of the business world is that successful people do take small steps toward reducing the degree of their weaknesses.

- While following your dream is important (because if you love what you do, the money will follow), it is equally important to know, for instance, if you want to start your own business that only one out of 15 companies survives. Out of the survivors, only one out of 15 makes it to the IPO stage of a stock offering. I've seen too many people jump into the market without having a rational plan for survival. Your journey will be challenging and long … but if it's what you love, that should ease the pain.

- Of course, the next best thing to overall happiness is business success or other areas of recognition. That sort of short-term success is similar to the feeling you get when you purchase a new car; it temporarily makes you feel good, and if handled properly, can be the platform for continued "happiness" analysis.

- Be rational about your passion, and then be passionate about your rationale. Then you'll increase your odds of matching what you love with your income.

- Please see the Illumination titled "Create Your Quest/ Architect Your Life" for more ideas on constructing "happiness and success" (www.warriorsalesmonk.com).

- You may wish to read <u>Authentic Happiness</u>, by Martin Seligman, Ph.D.

19. GRASS ALWAYS LOOKS GREENER

If the grass is greener on the other side of the fence, you can bet the water bill is higher.

ANONYMOUS

Start where you are. Distant fields always look greener, but opportunity lies right where you are. Take advantage of every opportunity of service.

ROBERT COLLIER

Is your grass less green because you've stopped watering?

TAZ

WHAT? Are you feeling like the grass looks greener at another company or a different industry?

SO WHAT? If you're considering leaving your job, and everyone does at some point, remember these two things.

- The real diamond mine may be in your own back yard. Remember that famous story from South Africa about the farmer who got frustrated about not making a good living in the farming business? He sold his farm and went prospecting for diamond mines. A few years later, one of the largest diamond mines was found on his former property.

- We all know people who have left jobs because they felt like the ship was sinking. However, years later, that same ship is fine and the person who left has changed jobs three more times.

NOW WHAT? Here are some real reasons to consider and score objectively:

- If you scored-above average on the Warrior dimension, you are more susceptible to "the grass looks greener" only at the times that you are on the edge of burnout. This occurs because you give every ounce of your energy to the achievement of the goal. If that goal is not attained or if you feel that your company didn't provide the resources or recognition attached to that goal, you're very disengaged on the job. You have become emotionally and physically drained and every little thing has now become a big deal.

- Here is a list of other reasons you may consider for leaving your company. If you check off more than four of these (and other people verify these things), you may have a reason to leave.

- Does your company have a culture that matches more with the Warrior or Monk dimension, but your dimension is opposite of their culture? Hmmm. This disconnect is a biggie. It may be time to assess looking for another opportunity.

- You don't get along with your manager.

- You don't believe in your solution.

- Is the market opportunity really there? (Are people buying your company's solution? Does your solution truly work for a business problem?)

- Have arbitrary rules and procedures become more important than results in your company?

- Do you feel you're not awarded or recognized enough (relative to other people in your organization) for things that you've done (and other people have commented on that)?

- Is recognition consistently purely political?

- Advancement is consistently blocked, and you're convinced that you want to get into management.

- Management is consistently poor in making strategic decisions.

- The company is not investing in you; after a long period of assessment, you truly can't connect "what you're doing today with your tomorrow."

- The manager consistently makes unreasonable demands.

- The amount of time spent on paperwork consumes at least 25% of your work day.

- The compensation structure does not match your personality (too much base and not enough "uncapped" potential, or too much on the commission and not enough base).

- The compensation structure is too difficult to be able to monitor your success at short-term and long-term intervals.

- The new commission plan changes dramatically (compensation program is designed to pay on growth, but you already have 90% market share in your territory).

20. GO AHEAD — SKIN YOUR KNEES, FALL OFF YOUR BIKE

We could never be brave and patient if there were only joy in the world.

HELEN KELLER.

You're going to make mistakes in life. It's what you do after the mistakes that counts.

BRANDI CHASTAIN, AMERICAN SOCCER OLYMPIC CHAMPION

It's not having everything go right, it's facing whatever goes wrong.

VICKIE M. WORSHAM

The things that hurt, instruct.

BENJAMIN FRANKLIN

A pearl is a beautiful thing that is produced by an injured life. It is the tear (that results) from the injury of the oyster. The treasure of our being in this world is also produced by an injured life. If we had not been wounded, if we had not been injured, then we will not produce the pearl.

STEPHAN HOELLER

WHAT? Failure is built into this game of life. Most of you will experience: cash-flow challenges; betrayals; accidents; unemployment; difficult managers; illness; a loved one's death; taxation without true representation; interpersonal relationship crisis; expectations not met.

SO WHAT? Yes, you need to experience small or large failures in order to move forward. The most interesting and the most successful people I know are the ones who have had challenges. They acquired knowledge and wisdom through pain. They got an effective MBA in the streets and not necessarily in the hallowed halls of academia. Entrepreneurial studies show that most entrepreneurs fail seven times before they make it big. These are people who understand that you have to strike out in order to hit a few homers. People always seem to forget the reality of that concept. Babe Ruth struck out 1,330 times, but hit 714 home runs. Michael Jordan didn't make his high school basketball team until his senior year.

I have personally seen companies make decisions about promotions based upon the candidate's experience with adversity and failure (compared to someone who just breezed through his or her job without challenges).

NOW WHAT?

- Don't beat yourself up over failures. Everyone has failures. Instead, focus on what you learned from that experience. Don't make that mistake again.

- Make sure that you get back on the bike.

- Get comfortable with the fact that possible "event" failures or short-term setbacks can be great learning grounds for long-term success. If you learn something each time that you fail, then you are closer to success!

21. LOVE THY COMPETITOR

The opposite of love is not hate but indifference.

-ELIE WIESEL

*Nothing is so strong as gentleness, nothing
so gentle as real strength.*

SAINT FRANCIS DE SALES

*Your product presentation is no match against
your customer's loyalty to the incumbent.*

TAZ

WHAT? Really? Really!!!

SO WHAT? Think about it. Do you have some competitors whom you don't like? Why? Do you add extra energy to any deal in which you're competing against them? Guess what – that's exactly how they are responding if they perceive that you don't like them.

If your competitors perceive that you personally don't like them, they will add more energy to try to crush you. Why would you want to provide them with motivation? Don't give them a reason to get up in the morning!

NOW WHAT?

- Be pleasant at the same time that you are professionally "kicking their butts."

- Take a lesson from the Italians, hold them close. Spend time chit-chatting with them about their background, their family and their interests. Learn as much as you can about them and try to uncover their motivations in life and in work. This is easy for me because I truly like people, and at the same time I like being fully informed about my business landscape.

22. MENTAL TOUGHNESS

In the second grade, they asked us what we wanted to be. I said I wanted to be a ball player, and they laughed. In eighth grade, they asked the same question, and I said a ball player, and they laughed a little more. By the eleventh grade, no one was laughing.

JOHNNY BENCH

The Only Easy Day Was Yesterday.

U.S. NAVY SEAL SLOGAN

Nothing in the world can take the place of perseverance. Talent will not; nothing is more common than unsuccessful people with talent. Genius will not; unrewarded genius is almost legendary. Education will not; the world is full of educated derelicts. Perseverance and determination alone are omnipotent.

PRESIDENT CALVIN COOLIDGE

I gain strength, courage and confidence by every experience in which I must stop and look fear in the face...I say to myself, I've lived through this and can take the next thing that comes along.

ELEANOR ROOSEVELT

WHAT? Navy SEAL training is considered the most arduous and challenging military training in the world. The slogan itself means that a true Navy SEAL (and in this case, a sales rep) understands that the only easy day is a day he or she has already gone through. This philosophy prepares you to handle challenges and stay focused on the goal.

SO WHAT? Regardless of your industry, sales is a dynamic and challenging profession. Preparing yourself mentally for the various challenges you will experience every day in sales will ensure you are building the mental toughness required to get out of bed every day and make effective sales calls.

Refining your mental toughness will allow you to manage your time, territory, accounts, and relationships effectively. And, it will allow you to compartmentalize things that are trying to emotionally hijack you and drain you of your energy that you need in order to make a great sales call!

Think about this: You're headed to an important meeting for which you have prepared extensively and the following events happen almost simultaneously: You receive two phone calls from existing customers who are requesting critical information immediately; you have two e-mails from new customers who need quotes yesterday; another e-mail hits your BlackBerry and it's a new player inside an existing customer requesting that you call immediately because they believe that you have been taking advantage of them (which isn't true and therefore indicates that a competitor has lied about you or your product and now there are people inside one of your accounts who are doubting your integrity); your manager just called and wants to speak with you about territory realignment (which you're concerned will reduce your income by 20%); your manager also told you that he needs your report by 5 tonight; and your wife just called and asked what time will you be home. By the way, your meeting starts in five minutes. Sound familiar? Now what?

At this point you need to focus on that immediate "25-meter HVT (High Value Target)" and stay on track for that meeting. Your mental toughness will allow you to "compartmentalize" and stay focused for your meeting. More important, you are ensuring that the flying monkeys that are waiting for your attention do not affect the outcome of your meeting. Furthermore, because your mental toughness has been refined to such an extent, you are already prioritizing your other issues in your subconscious mind and will be handling those issues adequately and professionally in a timely manner. (Even making your spouse happy!)

Mental toughness allows you to bounce back after a bad sales call or even career setbacks. Consider this: No one else is going to pick you up when a buyer says no; help you learn your products while at the same time that you're facing a huge sales target; help you learn your buyer's industry; or the skills of your profession. You just can't afford to be mentally soft and let those things derail you.

Success and mission accomplishment (closing deals) comes from hard work, persistence, and dedication (which all require mental toughness).

AND...

Actually, it's really not about mental toughness as much as it is about emotional toughness. Research shows that our "thinking" brain gets hijacked by our emotional brain when we encounter difficult situations. So, the reality is that mental toughness is acquired by not letting our thinking brain get hijacked. Emotional resilience is gained by letting your thinking brain override your negative emotions. By mentally preparing for difficult situations (visualizing), we increase our ability to emotionally deal with those situations if they manifest themselves (because we've already experienced them in our mind).

Unlike the Navy SEAL program, sales professionals do most of their mental toughness training on the job (unfortunately). So, ultimately, you have to realize that some sales calls are going to be your training ground (and learn from the experience). Focus on what you learned, not on the failure.

Acquiring emotional resilience/mental toughness has a psychological and behavioral component. For example: Trick the brain into believing that the buyer is not saying "no" to you as a person but rather is saying no to your presentation. If you take this psychological position, then your behavior remains calm and focused on finding a better way to communicate your solution.

NOW WHAT? Specifically, mental toughness helps equip us with the ability to be resilient in the challenging and rewarding world of sales. Expect to have challenges and obstacles. You have to know why you are fighting in order to help you continue to be resilient. Try the following to improve mental toughness.

- Compartmentalize your emotions, and therefore your focus, when situations present themselves that have the possibility of emotionally hijacking you. Focus on that immediate "25-Meter HVT." High value target (most people don't know this term

- Plan for the worst and hope for the best.

- Get comfortable with being uncomfortable (be prepared to suffer some injustices). Life is not always fair (in the short run).

- "Plan Your Dive, Dive Your Plan" (another Navy SEAL phrase). Research studies have shown that the most successful sales representatives in various industries spend a great deal of time PRE-call planning. Having a plan in place prior to your sales calls and doing your research will ensure a higher probability of success (you will feel more relaxed and competent and less likely to get stressed during the call).

- Make sure you have included contingencies in your plan, or "What if?" scenarios. For example, "What if the purchase agent asks me about prices or about the competition?"

- "Slow Is Smooth, Smooth Is Fast." Many times, we feel under pressure to do things quickly. This is when mistakes can be made. Focus on doing the job slow and smooth to ensure that you do not make mistakes. This could apply to product training, building proposals, gathering your thoughts for a big meeting, etc.

- It pays to be a winner! There can be both financial and personal victories associated with being mentally and emotionally resilient.

- Are you mentally tough enough to accept coaching? Are you coachable?

- Visualize achieving your objective and "capture" in your mind's eye how that will feel.

- Positive emotions help salespeople be successful. You have to be mentally tough enough to act and react from the position of love and gratefulness, no matter what the circumstance.

- Acquiring emotional resilience/mental toughness has a psychological and behavioral component. For example: Trick the brain into believing that the buyer is not saying "no" to you as a person but rather they are saying no to your presentation. If you take this psychological position, then your behavior remains calm and focused on finding a better way to communicate your solution.

- Avoid falling into self-delusion of grandeur or the pit of despair. This balance requires you to be self-aware, to be your own critic, to take constructive criticism from others, and the discernment to understand the difference between constructive criticism, destructive criticism or delusional criticism.

To learn more about overcoming obstacles and understanding the importance of resilience you may wish to read <u>The Victorious Personality</u> by Orison Swett Marden.

23. GET OVER IT

Everything can be taken from a man but one thing: the last of the human freedoms – to choose one's attitude in any given set of circumstances, to choose one's own way.

VIKTOR FRANKEL

No one can make you feel inferior without your consent.

ELEANOR ROOSEVELT

WHAT? Your buyers really don't care about you. Stop trying to define yourself and validate your existence by making sure that every buyer really likes you as a person.

SO WHAT? Wanting your buyers to like you as a person is a waste of your precious energy. There is not enough time for them to know everything about you. They will only see the part of you that is the "tip of the iceberg." The majority of who you are is below the water line. And, frankly, they don't care if you go to church, are a part-time coach, or if you are the president of the PTA!

What they *do* care about is how you will take care of them. How will you make *their* lives easier by simplifying their job or making them look good in their organizations and/or industries. Interestingly enough, the more you get to know and take care of your buyers, the more they will care about you as a person. (This may be the result, but this should never be your objective.)

NOW WHAT? Do the best job that you can, not for the sake of your customers or buyers liking you, but for the sake of yourself. Go the extra mile so that you can feel good bout the service you provide and the quality of work that you do.

24. ACTIVITY CREATES RESULTS

"If you can't fly, run. If you can't run, walk. If you can't walk, crawl. But by all means, keep moving."

MARTIN LUTHER KING, JR. (1929—1968)

AMERICAN CIVIL RIGHTS LEADER

NOBEL PEACE PRIZE WINNER

If I had to sum up in one word what makes a good manager, I'd say "decisiveness." You can use the fanciest computers to gather the numbers, but in the end you have to set a timetable and act.

LEE IACOCCA

You don't have to be physicist to know these truths: Inanimate objects have no momentum, and the greatest energy in the world comes from loose electrons.

TAZ

Study long, study wrong.

JOHN WILLIAMS, NATIONAL SALES MANAGER

WHAT? While planning is a key to success, some people tend to get stuck in the "virtual war games" mentality of problem-solving because they believe that there is one right way to solve a problem.

Sometimes the kissing cousin to planning is needed: to act swiftly and with conviction.

SO WHAT? An incredible amount of time is spent trying to determine the one way that will address a particular issue – viable options are tossed aside and credible elements of potential solutions are dismissed. More important, there are some things that are unknown until you put them into action and can see the reaction.

Many an opportunity has been lost because people are not quick enough. So much time is spent on discussing, planning, and organizing – making sure that every little detail is in place before they approach the customer – that the window of opportunity is missed. Someone else comes in cinches the deal – seemingly right from under you.

Lots of top-performing salespeople use "activities" as a way to collect more information and generate momentum. Examples of activities are: engaging with various "peripheral" players (i.e. support staff) inside the buyer's organization, inviting the buyer to industry conventions, and so on. Please see the Illumination titled "Your Best Day ... Scorecard."

NOW WHAT?

- Realize that there may be several "right ways" to do something – pick one or more and see them through.
- Don't be quick to dismiss suggestions that have been tried in the past.
- Look for elements of an approach that you may apply in different ways.
- Have more than one solution prepared to address a particular problem (options into actions).
- Try more than one approach in different areas and compare results.

25. MARSHMALLOWS AND SILVER BULLETS

Genius is 10% inspiration and 90% perspiration.

THOMAS EDISON

I was taught that the way of progress was neither swift nor easy.

MARIE CURIE

You may have to fight a battle more than once to win it.

MARGARET THATCHER

WHAT? The famous marshmallow study (from the Illumination "Reality Markers of Success") proved that happy adults are the ones who have learned to hold off immediate gratification. To augment that thinking, silver bullets have the potential to be a form of immediate gratification and at a minimum they are rare and are usually insidiously dangerous.

SO WHAT? There are times when organizations implement a "silver bullet" strategy and it actually creates more work down the road.

There was a businessman who presented himself as being able to place people in hard-to-find jobs. People paid money to use his service of high-powered job placement. Ultimately, in order to save time, this businessman did a cut-and-paste from monster.com for some of the jobs and eventually got a visit from the state attorney general (because his service fees were based upon allegedly false advertising of "hard to find jobs").

This businessman was using a silver bullet strategy to get his clients working on job opportunities. It saved him time in the beginning, but cost him big in the end.

All business concepts and strategies are diamonds in the rough. Over and over again, I've seen that the real work occurs when it's time to execute those strategies. After working with several start-up companies, and speaking with people who remained with those companies through hard times, I'm convinced that the right execution is just as critical and perhaps more rare than the right strategy. And, sometimes that silver bullet is not so shiny.

NOW WHAT?

- While looking for the simplest solution, it's important to be wary of the silver bullet. As my dad would say, "If the job is worth doing, it's worth doing right!"

- Ask yourself: Is this a self-discipline issue? Unfortunately, that ol' self-discipline challenge is both trite and inescapable.

26. THREE PILLARS OF CAREER SUCCESS

*I've met a lot of successful people in my life. They always
have these three traits: They work hard, they work smart,
and they get along with people. Like the legs of a stool, if any
of these three things are missing, they won't be successful.*

JOHN BROWN, CHAIRMAN OF THE BOARD, STRYKER CORPORATION.

*The marathon culture of "I work harder than you do" is
nothing but an excuse to avoid making the hard decisions*

SETH GODIN

If you want a job done, give it to a busy person.

ANONYMOUS

WHAT? The three pillars of career success are: work smart, work
hard, and get along with people. It is that simple and that complex.

SO WHAT? To a greater degree, I believe work-life balance is a
myth (especially if you are doing a job that is a stepping stone to finally
doing what you love to do … and once you start doing what you love
to do, work gets integrated into life but it still takes a lot of time). I
constantly see successful people putting in extra time compared with
the average person. However, they also find ways to work smarter as
well as find ways to effectively decompress. The superman bravado of
"look how hard I'm working" is really an excuse. There is even a book

titled The Superman Complex by Max Carey, describing this complex of people who have a belief system that "I can and should do everything" (and often times are left with nothing). I have always worked long hours regardless of whether I was passionate about a job or not (because I connected that job to future opportunities). Now that I am in my 40s, and I own my own business, I constantly strive to work smarter so that I can have the best of both worlds – I have the work ethic of my baby boomer generation, but I have the job-reasoning mentality of Generation X (seeking a life outside work during their early years of career development, even at risk of slower promotion opportunities). If you are passionate and confident in your work and personal life, you will spend time in accordance with your life priorities. You will work extra long hours when you need to and you will be able to spend time in personal life without feeling guilty in work life. And, the two "lives" will feed on each other in order to give you the energy you need to be satisfied in both areas of your life.

An example that is relevant for all of us is the scenario of starting a new job. When starting a new sales territory or taking over an existing sales territory, the best sales consultants work extremely hard at fulfilling all elements of getting "ramped-up." Eventually, however, the best reps start finding opportunities for working smarter. For example, when I was a sales manager, our team was calling on decision-makers who had busy Monday mornings (and all of our competitors were trying to call on them at the same time), but these same decision-makers had greater accessibility on Friday afternoons. I was bold enough to say to my team "for one month, take Monday mornings off but work Friday afternoons until 5 p.m." It was a huge success for driving new business.

When it comes to getting along with people, the best sales reps build fantastic relationships inside their own organizations. This allows them to get access to resources to help them compress and close sales cycles. They spend time "selling internally." Ross Perot (founder of EDS) is famous for many things, but many people lose sight of his selling career. When he was at IBM in the '60s, he would hit his quota for the year in 14-15 days after the annual quotas were announced!!! He always attributed an element of his success to building internal customers inside IBM.

NOW WHAT?

- One of the aspects of working smarter, is understanding that every person with whom you come into contact, inside your buyer's organization as well as inside your own organization, can make your life easier if you have built a good relationship with him or her.

- Your current work patterns may be ineffective. For example, start tracking how many calls convert to actual appointments as well as how many you convert from appointment to a sale. Then, look at the various components that affect your results: Are you identifying the right account (what is your lead generation tool); are you saying the right things to get the appointment? Do you have a process for moving people from being interested into actually being a customer? What is that process (see the Illumination "Nine Steps to the Competitive Conversion") and are you stalling at the same step every time? Are you picking the worst time of day and week to try to see your prospect?

- An example of working smarter is: Find out when the best time is to reach buyers (when are they least busy?). If it is Friday afternoons, take Monday mornings off (when 60 of your competitors are trying to contact them) to trade for making late-Friday-afternoon calls. This will increase your odds of making productive contacts.

- Another example of working smarter is getting along with people. If you get along with people, it can compress the amount of time that it takes for you to achieve short- and long-term goals. You have to be sensitive to different personality traits and how they perceive your main personality trait (see the TIGON assessment at www.warriorsalesmonk.com). Some people want to get down to business and some people want to chat. Can you recognize those personalities and adjust to make them feel comfortable? Do you treat everyone you meet like they are the CEO of your company (both customers, peers, and internal assistants)?

- Manage your activities, NOT YOUR QUOTA. Break down your quota into smaller chunks (e.g. your quota is not really $2M; since $1.4M is residual business, your quota is really $600,000). Then figure out your average sale price and how many current customers need to buy more, and how many competitive conversions you need to drive. Now, all of sudden, your number is really manageable. Once you have determined your targeted accounts, now you need to break down all the activities that need to be done (and do this by noting each activity in a timeline for that account) in order to complete the sale. If you focus on doing these activities well, you will hit your number!

27. THAT 10% THING

The majority of your competitors are focused
on being "just good enough.

TIM SMITH

Inches make champions.

VINCE LOMBARDI

At 211 degrees water is hot. At 212 degrees, it boils. And
with boiling water, comes steam. And steam can power a
train. The one extra degree can make all the difference.

SAM PARKER,

WHAT? Working 10% smarter, 10% harder, and focusing on getting along 10% better with other people is the productivity X factor.

SO WHAT? Seriously, it works. Taking time to be 10% smarter, 10% more effort into working harder, and putting 10% more time into getting along with all people (internal to your organization, your immediate customers, and the people who surround the immediate customers) pays off in business opportunities, commissions and promotions.

In one of our surveys, we asked the best salespeople if they had experienced the emotion of hating to make another call (at the end of the day) and if they had battled with quitting their work day before making that call or making one more call. Every one of them said that they had experienced that scenario.

Then we asked them about their results in which they did make that one more call. Every one of them said they had favorable results. Eight-five percent said they had excellent (the highest ranking) favorable results. Wow. That 10% thing does have an impact on your wallet.

Now what?

- Ask yourself: What are you willing to sacrifice to get what you want (by inputting the extra 10% effort)? Time, pride … but never your reputation or character.

- Push yourself to give the additional 10%. It really isn't all that much more than what you're doing now. It's the great separator from your competitors and peers.

- Start with getting along with people who are difficult. (Give yourself a point score for every time you make them smile or laugh. I used to do this with really "dry" or non-pulse-bearing purchasing agents.)

- Then move to working smarter. An example: Find out when the best time is to reach buyers (when are they least busy?). If it is Friday afternoons, take Monday mornings off (when 60 of your competitors are trying to contact them) to trade for making late-Friday-afternoon calls. This will increase your odds of making productive contacts.

- Smarter is … having a sales process like PAIDA™ and a key account process like the Matrix Sale (which identifies key players, enemies, champions, and motivations).

- Become even smarter by looking for patterns that are limiting your breakthrough performance (i.e. is every deal stalling out at a certain point in the sales process?). Take the time to figure it out and then fix it.

- Become smarter by creating unique customer interactions that help them remember you.

- Finally, move to "working harder." Make at least one more call a day; increase customer interactions and service experiences.

28. OVERNIGHT SUCCESS IS ONLY FOR FEDEX

*Human felicity is produced not so much by great
pieces of good fortune that seldom happen, as by
the little advantages that occur every day.*

BEN FRANKLIN

Overnight success is only for FedEx.

TAZ

*Is success a function of evolution or creationism? The research
is clear … it is more of an evolutionary process (that includes
experiencing failure) … a process of adapting for survival.
Small steps lead to success … not one big "bang" event.*

TAZ

WHAT? Success is created from a series of habits. The media and
the entertainment industry create a false impression of success. The
reality is that of the billions of people on Earth, maybe only six in
your lifetime have actually been just plain outrageously lucky (even
the majority of lottery winners end up going bankrupt). The majority
of successful people "look as if" they were lucky. In reality, they had
created a series of habits that eventually brought about their perceived
instant success.

SO WHAT? Umm, did we mention success? Success is groomed from your positive habits. Can we create habits? Yes, it is absolutely necessary. Why? Because we can't help ourselves!!!! Nine-five percent of human actions are subconscious; only 5% are conscious. We have to build habits in order to build into our automated actions. Do your habits reflect your values and belief systems so that you feel good about your day, week, month, life? How you plan and spend your time (habits) as well as your actions speak volumes of our values and your productivity.

Ben Franklin has had a major influence on human beings understanding habits or rituals. Ben Franklin contemplated the idea of habits and human behaviors from the position of trying to be more virtuous. He tracked his actions on a daily basis so that he could review his progress. He had a simple formula for increasing his virtues. Values into action = virtue

The following is a direct excerpt from the book Autobiography of Ben Franklin:

"The Precept of *Order* requiring that *every Part of my Business should have its allotted Time,* one Page in my little Book contain'd the following Scheme of Employment for the Twenty-four Hours of a natural Day,

I entered upon the Execution of this Plan for Self Examination, and continued it with occasional Intermissions for some time. I was surprised to find myself so much fuller of Faults than I had imagined, but I had the Satisfaction of seeing them diminish. To avoid the Trouble of renewing now & then my little Book, which by scraping out the Marks on the Paper of old Faults to make room for new Ones in a new Course, became full of Holes: I transfer's my Tables & Precepts to the Ivory Leaves of a Memorandum Book, on which the Lines were drawn with red Ink that made a durable Stain, and on those Lines I mark's my Faults with a black Lead Pencil, which Marks I could easily wipe out with a wet Sponge. After a while I went thro' one Course only in a Year, and afterwards only one in several Years … ."

All of us can achieve greater success via taking smaller steps, creating new habits, toward success. Ultimately, by having a game plan for adopting new habits, we dramatically increase the odds of adopting new behaviors. We need to construct these new habits as rituals into a work day because:

Disruptions will happen, and without a solid plan, we will be like a sailboat that knocks around without ever catching the wind.

NOW WHAT?

- Keep in mind, adopting new habits and behaviors takes only 10% inspiration but initially will require 90% perspiration (establishing a new behavior takes 23 days of repetition).

- Perform a 168 exercise. What is the 168? Time management meets the reflection in the mirror. The 168 is designed to look at an average week. 7 days x 24 hours a day equals 168!!

- Review your daily routines and assign daily time values to the following:

- Work (What am I really spending my time on? What habits are nonproductive? What new habits could help me produce more revenue?)

- Sleep (Do I need to get more in order to be healthy and alert?)

- Family time

- TV

- Now review your results and ask yourself:

- How am I spending my time?

- How can I possible fit all of this into my schedule?

- Do I have the free time I need to accomplish everything on my plate?

- Is my life managing me vs. me managing it?

- When you are finished, look at the areas you wish to highlight or to change (that you had noted on your daily dairy for the weekend and the week).

- Now, look at your daily itinerary and ask yourself "Where can I exhibit my values?" This helps take daily activities and habits and turns them into rituals.

- Keep in mind, the mark of a true performer is when you achieve your second and third year of quota attainment; an environment in which you ultimately competed against yourself!!!

29. TALENT: NOT ENOUGH

We are what we repeatedly do.

ARISTOTLE

Common sense doesn't mean that it is common practice.

CHARLIE JOHNSON, COFOUNDER OF META

The great thing about tomorrow? I can be better tomorrow than I am today.

TIGER WOODS

I have failed over and over again in life and that is why I have succeeded.

MICHAEL JORDAN

WHAT? Is it talent or "continuously executing a predetermined process" that separates performance? All of us have known people who have wasted their talent. We intuitively know that talent is just not enough. We all have seen less-talented people eclipse the performance of individuals who have more talent. But, is it possible for less-talented people to become top performers? In his book, *Talent is Overrated: What Really Separates World-Class Performers from Everybody Else,* author Geoff Colvin uses research to make a formidable and undisputable assertion that high achievers attain their status from "deliberate practice." At our consulting firm, we have case study and testimonials about the impact that a "repeatable sales process" can have on driving sales. Individuals use a process to identify key areas that can be improved and they increase their sales by deliberately focusing on a specific skill to be learned.

SO WHAT? The minute you start to get comfortable with thinking that you can just show up and get a sale, your performance has already started dropping.

NOW WHAT? Review the Illuminations that refer to sales process (PAIDA™) and tactics. Determine your weaknesses that exist inside those processes, and seek out sales coaching or additional books, subscriptions, magazines that focus on that topic. Reading this information is not enough; to develop a skill, you must apply it verbally, contextually and repeatedly.

30. SELLING MBA: KEY KNOWLEDGE AND SKILLS

Gather in your resources, rally all your faculties,
marshal all your energies, focus all your capacities
upon mastery of at least one field of endeavor.

JOHN HAGGAI

If people knew how hard I worked to get my
mastery, it wouldn't seem so wonderful at all.

MICHELANGELO

WHAT? Every profession has critical knowledge and skill categories that beckon for mastery. Knowledge is the science, and skill is the application of that knowledge. The sales profession has three main categories of knowledge and skill: sales process; psychology of the sale; and communication skills.

(1) SALES PROCESS:

Territory planning; annual business planning; quarterly business calibration planning; monthly activities planning; weekly activities planning; daily activities planning and pre-call planning (PAIDA™).

(2) PSYCHOLOGY OF THE SALE:

Part A: Your head

Are you in the right frame of mind to make this sales call? Are you motivated to have an impact for the customer and yourself? Get in the mood before your mood gets you!!!

Part B: Prospect's/Customer's head

> Dominant personality traits (i.e. expressive, driver, thinker, relater) are important for understanding how to build rapport and trust.

> Customer segmentation: Past purchase behaviors predict the future.

(3) COMMUNICATION SKILLS

Opening the call; benefit-feature statements; objection handling; "value" questions; uncovering emotional and rational buying motives; industry knowledge questions; demonstrating value; advancing the sale; etc.

SO WHAT? You now have indentified three key areas that are distinct to the sales profession. Master salespeople are like any other profession. The more knowledgeable and the more skilled (application of knowledge) you are will have a direct translation into higher income.

NOW WHAT?

- To get an MBA in selling, you must become familiar with the key knowledge and skill areas and determine your strengths and weaknesses. From that point, you completely demolish any weakness through collecting the knowledge and working on the application of that knowledge.

- Sales processes. Are you using the following processes: annual business planning process; territory planning; quarterly, monthly, weekly, daily and sales-call processes? If not, develop one using some of the material from this book.

- Psychology of the sale. Look at the last three purchases that your current prospects made that had nothing to do with your company (but were similar … e.g. capital equipment) and determine how they bought, why they bought, the criteria and the overall process. Did they buy out of budget? Now, from a much broader perspective, look at the last 10 sales that you have made and find the common denominators. Can you put those buyers into three to seven "buying styles or behaviors" (e.g. Stevie state of the art; analytical Allan; next year Ned)? Now, create questions that will help you identify which buying style fits for your current prospects and be prepared to implement an overall sales flow that will allow those with that buying style to buy the way they want to buy. Congratulations, you've just created a customer segmentation/psychographic profiling exercise that will compress your sales cycle and close more deals.

- Insight: Psychology of the sale is the one that is most overlooked but offers the greatest opportunity for advancing and closing the sale (if you uncover the buyers' emotional and retail motivators, they will move the sale along for you.)

- Learn more about dominant personality traits in order to increase your odds of influencing them (see the Illumination titled "The First Four Minutes").

- Communication skills. Do you have words and tone that: facilitate the buyers' understanding of benefit statements; objection handling; and advancing the sale? Study and find those words (some of them are in this book). The difference between "almost" the right word and the right word is the difference between a lightning bug and lightning.

31. IT'S OK TO TALK TO YOURSELF

I'm schizophrenic and so am I.

ANONYMOUS

A man should take away not only unnecessary acts but also unnecessary thoughs, for thus superfluous acts will not follow after.

MARCUS AURELIUS

WHAT? Talk to yourself as a form of performance improvement.

SO WHAT? Every successful salesperson or business owner (with a background in sales) has told me that they talk to themselves before sales calls or presentations. One aspect of talking to yourself is the idea that you can rewire your behavior or self-esteem issues by changing your talk tracks (being positive about yourself allows other people the opportunity to enjoy being around you).

Talking to yourself prior to meetings is critical. I found this to be one of the most effective ways to work on my delivery (not just the words I was going to say, but <u>how</u> I was going to say them). This process helps refine communication skills, helps anticipate any potential issues that buyers may have, and stops the rambling during the call. Ultimately, this practice allows you to be more relaxed when you're in the live call. Also, it is healthy and constructive when establishing positive talk tracks about yourself.

NOW WHAT? Start talking to yourself – right now ... I can't hear you!!!

32. STOP, DROP AND ROLL

An unexamined life is not worth living.

HENRY DAVID THOREAU

*A burning passion coupled with absolute
detachment is the key to all successes.*

MAHATMA GHANDI

*Your most unhappy customers are your
greatest source of learning.*

BILL GATES

WHAT? Have you heard firefighters teach children to "Stop, Drop and Roll" when there is smoke or fire? This sound advice also applies in the sales arena when things are hot and could potentially go up in flames. Take the time to stop and consider what it is that you are doing.

SO WHAT? The greatest minds have spent time reflecting in quiet places. Plato, Descartes (in warm ovens), da Vinci (lying down in fields while engaged in major projects), David Hawkins (in Wisconsin igloos). Contemplation allows you the opportunity to make sure that you are:

- Grounded (following your architecture or quest)
- Using your time efficiently by focusing on the right things

- Finding new ways to do things
- Taking care of yourself.

During a reflective session, I realized that one of my business activities needed to be revitalized and re-scripted. I was going through the motions of providing technical in-services to operating room nurses because I was of the belief that those nurses needed to be informed of how the product worked. Ultimately, it occurred to me that the primary reason I was there was to (1) build relationships and then (2) provide technical assistance. So, realizing that, the next in-service I did I provided fortune cookies for the nurses when they got the technical questions right. I became known as the fortune cookie guy and nurses would casually keep me informed of what my competition was doing! By putting extra time into them, they put extra time into me! This would not have happened if I had not reflected on the nature and real purpose of that business activity.

NOW WHAT?

- Turn off TV, the Internet, your phone, your computer. These are distractions that are keeping you from recharging your personal battery pack. For many salespeople, this can be done during "windshield" time.

- Are you consumed by tactical issues and to-do lists? While these are important, they require your attention to make sure that they are the right to-dos.

- Why are you doing certain business activities? What is the real reason for these activities? Accentuate the real reason and not the actual act of doing that activity (like the example noted above).

- What is your time worth? Are you dealing with things that need to be handed over to an expert (stocks, etc.)? Should you be letting the kid next door mow your lawn so that you can relax to recharge your battery for the more important things? All work and no relaxation lead to burnout.

- Review the last few days and consider how you could have made them more productive.

- Review the next few days and consider how you can make them more productive.

33. TIME MANAGEMENT: THREE DEADLY SINS

*The definition of insanity is doing the same thing
over and over but expecting different results.*

BENJAMIN FRANKLIN

It's not that you're busy, it's what are you busy with?

HENRY DAVID THOREAU

*It is not enough to have a good mind.
The main thing is to use it well.*

DESCARTES

WHAT? The three common mistakes every sales rep makes when it comes to time management are:

- Picking the wrong opportunity
- Focusing on the wrong player
- Choosing the wrong activities.

SO WHAT? If you are wasting valuable time, you are increasing your chances for missing your annual sales target. Many salespeople spend all their time chasing the "big account." The reality is that the big account is worthy of some of your time until it's worthy of more of your time. That happens when the account communicates that he or she has a need and you really have a shot at the business.

Our experience with top-performing reps is that they have already advanced the selling opportunities that are going to help them make their sales targets for the <u>next</u> year. They spend the right amount of time pursuing the right opportunities. In other words, they have learned to accurately prioritize and effectively manage their time.

A common time-waster is getting trapped into working with a buyer who loves you but doesn't have the power to get the deal done.

NOW WHAT? Understand that you need to stop spending all your time hunting elephants or calling on people who you know love you. You need to create a balanced effort between snacking on small opportunities (in order to gather momentum and build your baseline sales revenue) while taking bites out of the elephant.

WHO IS YOUR BEST PROSPECT?

A current customer is your best prospect since he or she already likes you, trusts you, and you know the customer's buying process. Review your current customers and determine the additional products, solutions or services that you could sell to them. And, if they have communicated that they have a "need," then this is the proverbial low-hanging fruit.

Your current customers can be broken into four categories (listed in order of importance): high-revenue potential and have communicated a need; lower-revenue potential and have communicated a need; high-revenue potential but haven't communicated a need; low-revenue potential and haven't communicated a need.

COMPETITIVE ACCOUNTS.

Once you've assigned your time to driving revenue from inside current customers, break down competitive accounts and use the same categories: high-revenue potential and have communicated a need; lower-revenue potential and have communicated a need; high-revenue potential but haven't communicated a need; low-revenue potential and haven't communicated a need.

Now, figure out how much time and effort to spend on each of these opportunities in a month's time. For example, one month is 20 business days. If you determine an account or an opportunity gets 30% of your time, it means you will spend six days out of the month on it (20 days x 30% = six days). Allocate a percentage to each account and/or opportunity, then translate that time into days or hours. See the sample chart below for a start.

Current Customers	Competitive Accounts
A). High-revenue potential; communicated a need Opportunity Name_____ $ % time: _____ Days/Hours_____	B). High-revenue potential; communicated a need Opportunity Name_____ $ % time: _____ Days/Hours_____
C). Lower-revenue potential; communicated a need Opportunity Name_____ $ % time: _____ Days/Hours_____	D). Lower-revenue potential; communicated a need Opportunity Name_____ $ % time: _____ Days/Hours_____
E). High-revenue potential; no communicated need Opportunity Name_____ $ % time: _____ Days/Hours_____	F). High-revenue potential; no communicated need Opportunity Name_____ $ % time: _____ Days/Hours_____

G). Low-revenue potential; no communicated need	H). Low-revenue potential; no communicated need
Opportunity Name_____$	Opportunity Name_____$
% time: _____ Days/Hours_____	% time: _____ Days/Hours_____

Now, on a separate piece of paper, list the accounts that you have put in the boxes in order from box A to box H. Here is the proper order of attack. When you have done this for each opportunity, further break down this time (days or hours) into activities by week. This is a great process to make sure that you're using your time effectively by focusing on the right opportunities.

34. PAIDA™ = PAYDAY

*AcSELLeration: Discipline to a predetermined
process of best practices.*

TAZ

*Winners have simply formed the habit of
doing things losers don't like to do.*

ALBERT GRAY

*Perfection is achieved not when there is nothing more
to add, but when there is nothing left to take away.*

ANTOINE DE SAINT EXUPERY

WHAT? Show me a high-performing sales organization, and I'll show you one that has a sales-call methodology or process.

SO WHAT? Following a process increases your competence and therefore confidence. At our consulting firm, we help our clients increase performance by first understanding the common denominators of every sales call.

If you use a repeatable process, it can help you: constantly assess your skill at every step of the process (so you can review and improve); compress the sales cycle, because you focus on the best practices during every sale; and stay cool even during stressful encounters (much like the military, after giving new recruits a process for firing a rifle, it then requires that they train with live ammunition in order to have them fight through stress and rely on their training). PAIDA™ is an example of a sales-call process.

If you follow a process, it will constantly remind you of the steps that are necessary before you make a sales call. For instance, if you don't take the time to put in an ounce of research, you may be spending pounds of effort that don't address the root cause of the situation. Keep your sales efforts healthy and apply an ounce of research, it will save you time and effort.

Here is something that Gary Summy, a director of training at Trane, had to say about preparation:

"I recently had an experience that brought the preparation component into the sales world for me. I was asked to come to sales office and help a sales team develop a strategy for winning a major bid for comfort and air-quality systems for a large hospital expansion. I got there early and the sales team was late returning from a call so I decided to do some basic Web research. I went to the Web site associated with the hospital and found the project. I spent about 30 minutes looking over the information. When the sales team arrived and we started reviewing their plans and activities, I realized their knowledge was limited to the formal specifications they received from the designer. I knew more about the business reasons for the expansion, the market positioning, the value and prestige associated with the expansion, and even some things about the application that were missing from the sales team.

"After we reviewed all my information … they had a completely different assessment of the project and the reasons behind some of the specifications.

"What I was able to gather in 30 minutes of business research uncovered aspects of the project that changed the priorities from one product line to a completely different focus. The team changed how they approached the project, and they realized that a completely different set of people would drive the final decision. In addition, they were able to reposition value in terms the customer had defined for the project and use the customer's language, not our technical description of the solution. We provided a solution that was directly linked to the customer's reasons for doing the project, not our ability to meet the designer's specification."

NOW WHAT? An old saying many of us heard as children was that an ounce of prevention was worth a pound of cure. Identify the key steps of every call (that fit your selling environment). Customize the following steps with sub-components under each step:

- **P**reparing for the sales call
- **A**pproaching the buyer
- **I**dentify the pain of the buyer
- **D**emonstrate the value of your solution
- **A**dvance the opportunity to the next level

Each of the aforementioned steps has some key communication strategies that will need to get built out (i.e. approaching the buyer, [create interest, create intrigue, etc.]; advancing the opportunity; [closing techniques; objection handling; etc.]). Most of our clients have at least four to seven items under each step.

35. CSI: Autopsy of the Call

Some people think a "bad sales call" is a victimless crime. That is simply not true. You are most likely the criminal and the victim.

TAZ

A properly constructed autopsy of a sales call will unveil many clues that will help stop future crimes.

TAZ

WHAT? Professional salespeople always look to improve their performance. The best take every opportunity to fully review each sales call in order to consider how to make future ones better.

SO WHAT? By doing an autopsy, you can reflect on how make future sales calls better and eventually you will reduce sales cycles, increase your closing ratio, and drive higher margins.

Now what?

- It is important that your autopsy begins as soon as the call is over. Much like crime scenes, some evidence (memory) gets lost if not addressed immediately.

- Ask yourself, "Self, tell me about the call?" What is the response you get back? Review what you did well, what you could better next time, and review the sales call to understand the buyer's needs and wants.

- The best autopsy follows a process: What happened at the beginning (getting started) of the call? How well did you build rapport? How good were your questions (did they uncover pain)? Did you listen well? Did you identify the next steps? How well did you handle any objections? Consider how you'd perform any of these skills better next time. You may want to use PAIDA™ as the process by which to review your sales-call performance.

36. WHY DON'T CUSTOMERS BUY?

The cemetery of lost deals has only eight headstones.

TAZ

WHAT? Losing a sale happens all too often. The cause: It's either them or you. Here are the common denominators associated with losing a sale:

THEM

- They don't like you.

- They don't trust you.

- They don't have a need or want.

- They don't perceive value in your product or service.

- They perceive that your solution is inferior to a competitor's.

- They are being pressured to use internal resources to solve the problem.

- They have no funds (and please don't take that at face value).

- They don't like the idea of change.

YOU

- You didn't engage their emotional or rational buying motives. You didn't help create "pain."

- No visibility to the customer's politics (every organization has some other department that has spent the money before your customer's department submitted its request).

- You didn't identify the real competitor (change? competitive rep loyalty? competitive company loyalty? internal departmental allocation of funds? nontraditional competitor, that is, some other product that has nothing to do with your solution, but is fighting for the same funding?) and then apply the right selling strategy.

- No visibility to the customer organization's true decision-making process.

- You never sold your value statements to the real decision-maker. You never identified the true champion.

SO WHAT? Umm, yeah. Did I mention "no sale?"

NOW WHAT? We've seen this happen too many times. All sales professionals we've consulted mention the following ways to keep your deals alive. They sound simple, and they are.

- Learn the science of rapport-building (see Illumination: "The First Four Minutes -- Dead on Arrival") to increase the odds of them liking you.

- Learn the science of creating trust. Tell them you are going to do something, and then do it. Create more "events or activities" to show that you're following up and doing what you said you would do. If you've got a deal on the table, work quickly to compress the time it takes to create trust (see the Illumination "Trust Treats (20/60/20)").

- Ask customers about other purchases that their departments or other departments (this will help you determine if you have an internal competitor competing for the same limited corporate funds) are planning, even if those purchases have nothing to do with your product.

- Ask your customers to "Help me understand the decision-making process that was used the last time that a purchase like this was made." Or, one of my personal trademark favorites, look at a recent purchase they made that has nothing to do with your solution, and ask them: "How did that get in here?" This helps you drive toward an understanding of their decision-making process and uncovering the real decision-maker.

- Ask at least seven people inside the organization, "Who will make the final decision on this?" You may get some different names, but look for a common denominator.

- Uncover, create and develop the pain. Leverage emotional buying motives (EBM) and be able to articulate rational buying motives (RBM).

37. YOUR REAL COMPETITION

You have visibility to only two of your four competitors ... no wonder we don't close more opportunities.

TAZ

I'm not in competition with anybody but myself. My goal is to beat my last performance.

CELINE DION

The truth is, there is nothing noble in being superior to your fellow men. True nobility lies in being superior to your former self.

WHITNEY YOUNG, CIVIL RIGHTS LEADER

WHAT? Master salespeople understand competition. They understand that competition is really captured inside four different buckets.

1st level of competition is <u>YOU</u> (first be best ... then be first). Will Rogers said: "Even if you are on the right track, you will get run over if you just sit there."

2nd level of competition is <u>change</u> (and there are two types of change that require a different approach).

> (A) Are you competing against the loyalty that the incumbent salesperson has built with the buyer?

(B) Are you competing against human beings' natural tendency to hate change? The fact is that buyers, like most humans, don't like change. Is the change you represent more about the product features or more about the buyer organization's having to learn something new (a new functional way to work with your solution), and they are comfortable with what they have?

3rd level of competition is <u>nontraditional</u> (any other product or solution that is pursuing budget dollars inside your buyer organization is ultimately competing against you).

4th level of competition is <u>traditional</u> (the products that you consistently compete against).

SO WHAT? If a buyer asked you for a pen, would you hand him or her a watermelon? Of course not!!!! However, you are unconsciously doing that when you engage in competitive tactics that don't match against the real competitor. You are harming your reputation with the buyer (wasting his or her time) and just as important you are wasting your time (i.e. you are competing against the buyer's loyalty to the other salesperson, but your response to that situation is to compete by giving a product feature and benefit presentation!?).

Your company hired you because it believes that you will always be focused on level 1. Your superiors expect that you will be constantly working on your game … and they were right because you are reading this book!!!!

Your company spends a lot of time and resources helping you understand the competitive products features and benefits (level 4 of competition). However, most people are not trained on how to deal with the more insidious and difficult competitors (level 2 and level 3).

The ability to effectively address these levels of competition is what separates average salespeople from master salespeople.

NOW WHAT?

- 1st level of competition is <u>YOU</u> (first be best ... then be first). Are you reading at least two books a year and or trying at least two or three new skills a year?

- 2nd level of competition is <u>change</u> (and there are two types of change that require a different approach)

  - Are you competing against the incumbent salesperson (the loyalty he or she has developed with the buyer)? Your best tactic is to love your competition. Why? Because your buyer loves that salesperson. Every time you speak with the buyer, he or she will smile and be pleasant, but will never move forward with you no matter how good your presentation. Worst of all, the buyer will never really give you critical information because he or she doesn't really want you to win. So, here is a six-step plan to convert this competitive situation.

  - Whenever you're talking with the buyer, make sure you glowingly speak about the competitive salesperson: "Rick is such a great guy and what a great family."

  - Mention to the buyer that "I know you'll never buy from me as long as Rick is your salesperson. I think it's great that you have that much loyalty."

  - After five sales calls in which you were glowingly speaking of Rick, you finally say, "I know that I'm never going to sell anything to you, but I would like to build a loyal relationship with my other accounts. What is it about Rick that has made you so loyal?" The buyer isn't going to give you the sincere answer if you haven't done a good job of steps 1 and 2. When he or she tells you, make a mental note and later jot it down.

- Four weeks later, casually say, "You know, I was thinking about your situation … and if Rick ever gets promoted or changes jobs, then what are you going to do? I was wondering if you would consider giving me a tryout to see if I'm worthy of being your Number 2? If I were to service just this one product [worth $75,000], Rick would still have $500,000 worth of business, but you could see if I'm worthy of your loyalty as a backup plan for you and your business."

- When you get the "tryout," every time you deliver something for the buyer, you ask if this matched his or her expectations, and be specific by asking "Was I responsive, on-call, and efficient?" (By the way, those were the words that the buyer used to describe Rick!!!)

- Are you competing against pure change? The fact is that buyers, like most humans, don't like change. Is the change more about the product features or more about the buyer organization's having to learn something new and the people are comfortable with what they have.

- If it is product features and benefits, you will need to be very clear on how this solution is better.

- If they are not interested in changing because of the hassle of change (they have gotten comfortable with all the processes of using the competitive product; it's not really the product, it's just easy to keep using the product), then you will need to really understand what is the concern about change. Here are some examples: the fear of losing something of value; misunderstanding of change; disbelief in change; low tolerance for change (don't want to change current comfort); risk/reward ratio is not big enough; management doesn't support change as a strategic initiative; the buyer doesn't feel pain … and this is the big one!!! Without pain, you can't move forward!!!

- You need to be sure that you have uncovered enough pain in order to have them consider changing. Here is a great formula to use:

  - **P + V + EA = change**

    - Pain + vision (for pain removal) + ease of adoption (how easy to implement) = change

- 3rd level of competition is <u>nontraditional</u> (any other solution that is pursuing budget dollars inside your buyer organization could end up impacting your ability to make a sale). You don't have visibility to the needs that other departments have inside your buyer's organization. I have seen deals get lost because, at the last minute, another department politically "stole" money from my buyer's departmental budget. Your plan of action here is to ask early on, "What other purchases are you considering in the next eight months? What are other departments requesting?" You need to be prepared to talk about how your solution impacts the strategic, key business drivers for your buyer's business. What you are doing is setting up the nontraditional competitor to be viewed as a "functional" need and not a strategic need (i.e. "My solution will help you drive more revenue, whereas that other product you mentioned will only incrementally help contain costs.").

- 4th level of competition is <u>traditional</u>. Yes, you need to know the differences between the feature, function and benefits of your product and your competitors' product. However, you also need to watch for the overall behaviors/processes that your competition uses in order to compete against you!! For example, I had a company that was a $50M division inside a $5B parent company. Its next closest competitor had $20M in sales. The competitor started flying in five of its executives (in suits) to be involved in every deal in order to show that it was committed and so that it wouldn't look so small. When caught in this situation, we counseled our client to respond to the buyers by saying, "Instead of flying all of our executives in to meet with you, we are taking that money, as well as the additional funding from our $5B parent company, and investing it into the next version of software as well as expanding our service teams. Quite frankly, if our executives had that much time to spend flying in for every opportunity, I'd be concerned about our future innovations!!!" Within two months, the competition stopped this tactic.

38. THE FIRST FOUR MINUTES
– DEAD ON ARRIVAL

There is a scene in <u>Tommy Boy</u> when Chris Farley lights the toy antique car on the buyer's desk. Just before that happens, David Spade is rattling off a series of technical terms and the buyer says "Whoa son, you're not speaking my language."

FROM THE FILM *TOMMY BOY*

Can you hear me now?

VERIZON COMMERCIAL TAGLINE

WHAT? Most research shows that buyers decide whether they like us in four minutes or less. Tired of blank stares? Wonder why people interrupt you? Puzzled by those who still want more information? Wish some people would stop finishing your sentences? Have you counted to 10 hoping someone would just "spit out" what they want to say so you can start talking again? Have you ever felt as if you never connected early in the conversation and it just got worse from there?

As salespeople we often love to talk, but do we present ideas in a way others can hear us?

SO WHAT? If we don't connect with them in the first four minutes, it doesn't matter what we say for the next 20 minutes. Also, if we can connect with them then, we can compress the sales cycle. As sales professionals, we are in the business of communication. So, we make the mistake of spending a lot of time on what we are going to say rather than on building the critical rapport to make sure that the buyer is receptive. We spend more time polishing our presentation then we do on CONNECTING with them in a way that ensures that they are readily receptive. We must make them comfortable with us before we make them comfortable with our message. When you concentrate on understanding the buyers' communication preferences (the radio station that they are tuned into … what music station is playing on their metaphorical headset?) and adjusting your style to them, it is amazing how some of the common communication frustrations fade away. Why? Presenting ideas in the manner people prefer to hear them (that is closest to their style) helps them relate to what you are expressing. For example, if one observes a customer talks fast and says "just give me the bottom line" and the salesperson keeps talking on and on about the product's many features, one has lost the client. The customer becomes impatient and we then tend to talk more, so the cycle only gets worse. When you recognize the buyers' communication preference clues and then adapt your style of communication to the buyers' style, then the communication really rocks.

NOW WHAT? Compress the sales cycle!! Diagnose the customer's dominant personality trait and sell to that trait. Be a chameleon (and versatile). Mirror the person with whom you are speaking. Your customer's comfort level increases with the similarity of your body language and speech. To mirror those effectively, we need to explore the science of dominant personality traits.

There is a science to rapport-building and that science is based upon reading people's dominant personality trait. Personality assessment is more than 2,000 years old and has become a gold standard for classically trained salespeople. To understand how to read people and communicate with them using their personality style preference, we must become a doctor of personality assessment by first diagnosing our buyer and then providing treatment. In D. Forbes Ley's book <u>The Best Seller</u>, he outlines the four main dominant personality types (Amiable Relater, Expressive, Driver and Thinker Analytical). Keep in mind, all of us have parts and pieces of all these types ... however, we all have a sweet spot that is our dominant personality type (DPT). Go to www.warriorsalesmonk.com and take the TIGON personality assessment to learn about your DPT.

DIAGNOSING PERSONALITIES:

The diagnosing process assessment begins with an understanding that there are two key measuring dimensions:

- An individual's responsiveness to other human beings (this is an axis that goes from south to north on the following graph). The scale looks like this: Walk into a party and stand by yourself (southern part of the axis); walk into a party and talk to just one or two people (middle part); walk into a party and talk with everyone, as well as leave having made two new friends (northern part of axis).

- Your desire to assert yourself in your environment (this is the axis that goes from east to west).

DOMINANT PERSONALITY TRAITS

Amiable Relater	High Responsiveness Personable Wants to be liked			Expressive (Socializer)
Intent: To be Supportive				Intent: To Persuade
Key: Reduce Conflict				Key: Their Ego
Motto: Can I help you?	**Personality Traits** Needs people	**Personality Traits** Dreamer		Motto: Let's Do It!
Wants: Peer Acceptance	Listener Status Quo	Unrealistic goals Creative		Wants: Applause for greatness
Time: Now is Never	No risks No pressure Counselor Focus on Feelings	Flighty Needs Approval Generalizes Persuasive		Time: Now is Next Week
Low Assertiveness	Supportive Less goal focus No conflict Soft hearted/kind	Opinionated Fast Decisions Excitable Enthusiastic		High Assertiveness
Avoids Risks				Job Oriented
Needs to	**Personality Traits** Planner	**Personality Traits** Goal Oriented		Fast Tempo
Follow	Slow Decisions Technical Must be right	Impatient Workaholic Demanding		Driver (Director)
Thinker	Conservative Organizer Low pressure	Decisive Time effective Blunt		Intent: To Overcome
Intent: To Avoid Trouble	Logical Precise	Administrative Opinionated		Key: Impulsive & Impatient
Key: Preciseness	Problem Solver Persistent	Innovative Tough		Motto: Get It Done, Yesterday!
Wants: Activity	Low Responsiveness			Wants: Results
Time: Now is Next Month	Disciplined			Time: Now is Now

The Best Seller. D. Forbes Ley

How well did you understand that last section? Take this quick assessment and see:

Match the adjectives to the personality type below

A	B	C	D
Detail-oriented	Sentimental	Action-oriented	Animated
Precise	Appreciative	Strong-willed	Enthusiastic
Logical	Even-tempered	Adventurous	Dramatic
Diligent	Agreeable	Competitive	Talkative
Technical	Cooperative	Impressive	Spontaneous
Thorough	Accommodating	Challenging	Stimulating
Accurate	Supportive	Powerful	Lively
Consistent	Patient	Candid	Popular
Orderly	Generous	Self-reliant	Optimistic
Quiet	Understanding	Aggressive	Outgoing
Trait:	**Trait:**	**Trait:**	**Trait:**

Diagnosing the Dominant Personality Trait

Diagnosing the Driver

Behavior Pattern	Self/Contained/Direct
Appearance:	Businesslike/Functional
Work Space:	Busy, Formal, Efficient, Structured
Pace:	Fast/Decisive
Priority:	The Task, The Results
Fears:	Loss of control
Under Tension Will:	Dictate/Assert
Seeks:	Productivity
Needs to know (benefits):	What it does; by when; what it costs?
Achieves acceptance by:	Leadership/Competition
Likes you to be:	To the point
Wants to be:	In charge
Irritated by:	Inefficiency/Indecision
Measures personal worth by:	Results, Track Record, Measurable progress
Decisions are:	Decisive
Risk approach:	Risk Taker

Diagnosing the Expressive

Behavior Pattern	Open/Direct
Appearance:	Fashionable/Stylish
Work Space:	Stimulating/Personal/Cluttered/Image
Pace:	Fast/Spontaneous
Priority:	Relationships: Interacting
Fears:	Loss of prestige
Under Tension Will:	Attack/Be sarcastic
Seeks:	Recognition
Needs to know (benefits):	How it enhances their status; who else uses it
Achieves acceptance by:	Playfulness/Stimulating environment
Likes you to be:	Stimulating
Wants to be:	Admired
Irritated by:	Boredom/Routine
Measures personal worth by:	Acknowledgment/Recognition/Applause/Compliments
Decisions are:	Spontaneous
Risk approach:	Risk taker

Diagnosing the Relater

Behavior Pattern	Open/Indirect
Appearance:	Casual Conforming
Work Space:	Personal/Relaxed/Friendly/Informal
Pace:	Slow/Easy
Priority:	Relationships: Maintaining
Fears:	Confrontation
Under Tension Will:	Submit/Acquiesce
Seeks:	Attention
Needs to know (benefits):	How it will affect their personal circumstances
Achieves acceptance by:	Conformity/Loyalty
Likes you to be:	Pleasant
Wants to be:	Liked
Irritated by:	Insensitivity/Impatience
Measures personal worth by:	Compatibility with others; depth of relationships
Decisions are:	Considered
Risk approach:	Avoider

Diagnosing the Thinker

Behavior Pattern	Self/Contained/Indirect
Appearance:	Formal/Conservative
Work Space:	Structured/Organized/Functional/Formal
Pace:	Slow/Systematic
Priority:	The task: The process
Fears:	Embarrassment
Under Tension Will:	Withdraw/Avoid
Seeks:	Accuracy
Needs to know (benefits):	How to justify the purchase logistically; how it works
Achieves acceptance by:	Correctness/Thoroughness
Likes you to be:	Precise
Wants to be:	Correct
Irritated by:	Surprises/Unpredictability
Measures personal worth by:	Precision/Accuracy/Activity
Decisions are:	Deliberate
Risk approach:	Avoider

Now, take a minute and test yourself to see if you can put your knowledge into action.

PERSONALITY TRAITS – MY TOP FIVE CUSTOMERS AND TOP THREE PROSPECTS:

PUT YOUR CUSTOMERS IN A BOX

Amiable Relator	Expressive
Analytical Thinker	Driver Director

Top five customers:	Top three prospects:
1. **Example:** Expressive	1.
2.	2.
3.	3.
4.	
5.	

Ask yourself, "Why did they fit here? Am I sure? What questions do I need to ask myself to be sure that they fit here?"

How to Treat Their Dominant Personality

Strategy	Driver	Expressive	Amiable Relater	Analytical Thinker
Getting the appointment	• Call • Send letter to confirm and brief fact sheet	• Call • Stress personal service	• Letter with a personal touch • Stress positive impact on customer	• Factual letter asking for appointment
Opening the call	• Be formal • State purpose • Quick pace • Provide info	• Informal; describe call purpose • Share stories of people they know • Quick pace	• Engage in informal chit chat first • Probe for their objectives • Ask about their customers	• Provide written info about your product and company • Acknowledge expertise of analytical • Show track record
Identifying need	• Probe directly • Clarify priorities • Show how you can support their goal	• Ask about expected outcomes • Listen and show support	• Create cooperative environment • Listen and give feedback • Want guarantees; show success stories	• Asking systematic questions • Stick to the facts • Ask their opinion based on facts
Advancing the sale	• Share case studies • Counter objections with case histories	• Don't rush discussion • Emphasize new technology • Who is using this new solution (image-conscious)	• Define solution • Provide lots of assurance • Mention others they could discuss it with • Have their staff brought in prior to meeting	• Provide lots of facts; outcomes info; pros and cons • Avoid emotional appeals • Don't rush them; give them time to study the issue and options
Requesting the referral	• Ask directly • Explain what you will do with referral	• Ask in a casual manner • Use "third-party influence" to overcome objections	• Don't push; ask indirectly • Stress your personal involvement • Encourage them to talk to others	• Don't ask on the first visit • Ask directly, but low key • Answer objections with facts; acknowledge their concern
Follow-up	• Provide feedback with short voice- or e-mail • Touch base intermittently	• Do something fun for person • Frequent contact; lots of attention	• Frequent contact • Card, flowers, candy for staff	• Regular short contact • Provide newest information
Do's and Dont's	• Do not be indecisive • Get to the point	• Do not bore them with details • Speak with confidence	• Do what you say you will do • Want to hear solutions, not problems	• Do not need to like you to buy from you • Never state a fact or feature without stating the benefit

Take the time to answer the following questions:

- Do you know your own communication style? Do you start conversations by "getting down to business" and speaking in bullet points? Or do you spend a lot of time talking about personal things (e.g. how was your weekend?)?

- How do you prefer to be talked with?

- You need to adjust your communication style to match your buyer's personality trait. For example: If you identified one of your customers as an "expressive" style, he or she will want to focus on just the main points and will have little patience for minor details. The customer would prefer exciting and creative sales presentations rather than slow ones with a ton of minutia; and wants to be friendly and prefers a casual environment. He or she loves taking risks and loves the new and innovative.

  Probes for this person would be:

  Am I right in assuming you will make the final decision?

  I feel I can work with you on this, how do you feel about me?

  Shall I take care of the paperwork for you?

  Many of your colleagues would feel the same way about this product, don't you agree?

  I can see you are a decisive person so which option should WE go for?

(Other examples of probes are at www.warriorsalesmonk.com.)

- Do you know that others' styles can be quite different from yours in pace, content and length?

- Do you observe how some people talk just about the task at hand and others want to focus on the people aspects of the sale?

- What have those closest to you told you about how you come across? Too talkative? Too much detail? Too challenging? Too analytical? Too modest?

- Have you tried adjusting your style to people around you? The most important thing is your ability to be versatile (i.e. chameleon) when talking with buyers, in order to match their style to your delivery.

- Have you taken a self-assessment of your own style? Many quality ones are available. TIGON is available at the Warrior Sales Monk Web site.

- Have you just stood back from your customers and observed how they express themselves? Observe any changes in their body language or speech that indicate excitement or displeasure.

- Make sure that the prospect or customer is mentally and emotionally prepared to have a conversation with you. Ask them: "Is now still a good time to talk?"

BOTTOM LINE:

People want to be talked with in ways they can relate to.

Take a look at yourself and make sure that you are matching your customer's communication styles.

To learn more, we offer flash video examples of their traits at www.warriorsalesmonk.com.

39. FOUR LANGUAGES OF VALUE

The value of something is a personal experience. Price is what you're willing to pay for that experience.

TAZ

WHAT? There are four different types of values that people want to experience when they purchase your solution. They are valuable to the buyers because they are currently experiencing the perception of pain/loss in these categories:

- Strategic value: Your solution will help them achieve their organization's top three corporate business objectives (for larger businesses, these would be noted in their annual report and may include things like increased market share, increased margins, etc.) or top three key business drivers (for smaller businesses, these are usually going to be marketing, sales, or long-term cost containment).

- Financial operational value: Does your solution reduce their operational expense or provide a clear ROI in the short term?

- Job or end-user value: Does your solution provide technical or functional advantages to the end user?

- Personal value: Does your solution allow the key player to achieve some personal wins (emotional buying motives – promotion, bonus, look smart, return a favor, etc.)?

SO WHAT? The general rule of thumb is that you need to be able to communicate how your solution can deliver on at least two of these value languages in order to get the sale. You must learn the language of these different values (by using the descriptive words noted above). There is a CAD/CAM (computer-aided design/computer-aided manufacturing) software company that drove sales dramatically by communicating a personal-value language to the key engineering influencers ("If you get trained on this software, it will make you more marketable for future job opportunities.").

NOW WHAT?

- Consider your current customer base. What are the common strategic value themes (market share, increased margins, increased referrals, etc.) that caused the last eight customers to buy? What are the common financial/operational themes? What are the common "end user" value themes? And what are the common personal themes? Once you find those common themes across all values, then you can probe buyers by asking questions that dive specifically into those themes (e.g. "In speaking with a lot of companies in your industry, they are struggling with capturing market share, increasing margins, and overworked employees ... are any of those true for your company?")

- Another way to look at it is to understand how your solution relieves the pain across four different levels of impact by reviewing your last eight customers to determine why they bought. Once you know why the last eight customers bought, you can build a hypothesis for "why future customers would buy." Example:

	Job	Financial	Strategic	Personal
Customer	Increase employees safety	Reduce insurance	Tell marketplace about employee safety and attract future talent	Feel good about taking care of your employees and coworkers

40. TRUST TREATS (20/60/20)

Follow-up is critical for establishing a short-term and long-term relationship.

TAZ

Kindly words, sympathizing attentions, watchfulness against wounding men's sensitiveness – these cost very little, but they are priceless in their value.

F.W. ROBERTSON

"Show me you care and then I'll share."

TAZ (ON BEHALF OF ALL BUYERS)

WHAT? Gaining trust with our buyers is a key to advancing the sale.

SO WHAT? Buyers will buy from people they trust. In general, in most sales territories, the following formula exists: 20% of the buyers will like you immediately; 60% will want to "wait and see"; and 20% won't buy from you in the next 18 months (expanded from The Best Seller by D. Forbes Ley). Where is the greatest opportunity for your territory? It lies within the 60% who are waiting to see!!!!! What are they waiting to see? They want to know that they can trust you!!!!!

When it comes to building trust, the buyer is unconsciously walking through the following formula: Am I comfortable with you in a casual conversation? Are you sincere to my pain? Have you shown me that I can trust you?

And a real-world story from Dirk Waedekin (see his bio at the end of this book): "I feel customers buy with trust, but also because of a sales-person's competence with their solution and their sincere listening to their customers concern or pain. As a field trainer, I can unfortunately recall times when a salesperson was not prepared for specific questions about his/her product and the buyer tuned out and was verbally and nonverbally questioning the 'sales professional' in front of him. The sale was not only lost, but retracted a few steps backward."

And, as far as listening to your customers to identify their pain or concern, I vividly recall a doctor's appointment (great doctors are great communicators) I went on with my wife (who had ongoing headaches and was tired all the time) with a family doctor. Obviously, we were concerned and had some questions. This particular doctor showed no concern, asked a couple mundane questions, performed a quick examination, and was getting ready to write a prescription before we had a chance to ask any questions. We both thought it was a little strange after we left the office and we were both taken aback by the doctor's lack of concern, which I found surprising because he was rated as the top doctor in his field by a leading heath-care magazine, and we were prepared to tell everyone and anyone that he was not a good doctor for you to see. He was not "sincerely" engaged in understanding her pain.

Now What?

- Develop and implement some Trust Treats early and often during the sale, things that you can do and say to help build trust (see the next bullet points).

- Are you competent with articulating your solution?

- Do you have good listening skills to be able to show your buyers that you are sincerely engaged in listening to their needs (see the Illumination "The Therapist Is In (Listening Skills").

- Research shows that trust can be gained from the buyers' experiencing your follow-up skills. They gain more trust as you continue to follow-up with their requests. A request is a buyers' "event" or activity that requires you to provide information or resources to help them do their job. It takes about six months to create trust. Why? Because it may take that long to have enough events to trust you. So, the key is to compress trust by creating more activities that require you to have to follow-up (i.e. "There was an interesting article in your industry trade journal about _____ ... I'll forward that article to you.").

- Put something extra on the proposal and then take it off within the first three minutes of the meeting. "I've been thinking about this on the way over and you really don't need 20 dozen, you probably only need 15 dozen."

- When negotiating, use very specific numbers: "I can only give you an additional 2.37% discount" versus saying "I can give you another 5%".

- Under-commit and over-deliver. Give 'em more than they asked for ... and make sure that you are doing it at the right time (e.g. train yourself to give the best for last). Here are areas to provide additional commitments or service: beat expected delivery dates; provide more training then originally agreed upon; cost – at the last minute, provide them free product or a slightly higher discount (not much) – they will trust you in all future dealings and give you future business opportunities; quantity of product or service agreement; warranty – extend it; any other extras????

- One of my favorites, tell them why they shouldn't do business with you!!! I have personally closed $1M deals with this Trust Treat. The reason is that they immediately stop worrying about the fact that you're trying to "sell them" or that you are desperate for the sale. The buyers will lower the walls and your chances of determining their needs go up dramatically. In the first few minutes you could say "I know we're both busy, so let me tell you why you might not want to do business with me"; "We're not a start-up company like a lot of other solutions out there that will present the fact they will customize every little thing. We're an established brand that is financially sound and provides the industry standards." Or: "Our solution is not the cheapest (we're the least expensive but not the cheapest)"; "Our solution requires that your people will need to participate in a 30-minute in-service, and if you feel that will be difficult for your team, then we shouldn't waste each other's time"; "Please don't purchase our solution if you think that there will never be a hiccup … all of your possible solutions are man-made and at some point in time they will have problems … (that is why we have the largest service team in the marketplace)." HINT: Never make the reason "why you shouldn't do business with me" a reason that they truly care about.

41. READ THEIR MINDS: GO PSYCHO

*I have always thought the actions of men the
best interpreters of their thoughts.*

JOHN LOCKE

Action is eloquence.

WILLIAM SHAKESPEARE

Don't listen to their words, fix your attention on their deeds.

ALBERT EINSTEIN

WHAT? Stop making your buyers such a mystery. Past purchase behaviors are the greatest predictors of their future behaviors.

SO WHAT? Their past purchases give you a window to their thought processes. It will give you the night vision to the reasons they bought, the criteria they used to make their selection, and the process (e.g. who was involved, who was the key decision-maker, did they buy out of budget, why did they buy out of budget?). Armed with this information, you can help your buyers buy the way that they want to buy. This, in turn, will shorten your sales cycle and increase your propensity for success.

NOW WHAT?

- Review your last 20 purchases and come up with three to five different types of psychological buyer behaviors and give them nomenclature: Stevie State-of-the-art (always wants something new); Alan Analytical (wants a ton of data before making a purchase); Sally the Servant (wants staff to be happy), etc.

- Once you determine how they want to buy (their psychological profile), now tailor your sales messaging to that type of profile: Stevie State-of-the-art, "this is the latest technology available;" Alan Analytical, "here are the exact specs and 9 out of 10 consumers have bought our product because of the three gigabytes and the safety-recovery mechanism;" Sally the Servant, "your staff will love you for making their life easier."

- Some good probes to uncover their past purchase behaviors.

  - Physically point to a similar object or solution and ask, "Wow, how did that get in here?" It doesn't even have to be the same product set, just another piece of capital equipment or software, etc. You can then ask, "What was the criteria for that solution? Who was involved in that decision?"

  - Ask the question, "In the past, when you have bought something similar, what was the process?"

  - Ask, "In the past, when you had to buy 'out of budget,' how did you get the funds?"

42. CREATING A UNIQUE CUSTOMER EXPERIENCE

Kindly words, sympathizing attentions, watchfulness against wounding men's sensitiveness — these cost very little, but they are priceless in their value.

F.W. ROBERTSON

Talk to a man about himself and he will listen for hours.

BENJAMIN DISRAELI

That you may please others you must be forgetful of yourself.

OVID

Validate people's existence by giving them your undivided attention.

TAZ

People don't care how much you know until they know how much you care.

DAVID EHRENBERG

No act of kindness, no matter how small, is ever wasted.

AESOP

While everything may be better, it is also increasingly the same.

PAUL GOLDBERGER, "THE SAMENESS OF
THINGS," THE NEW YORK TIMES

*"Pretend that every single person you meet has a sign around
his or her neck that says, 'Make me feel important.'"*

MARY KAY ASH (1918–2001)
AMERICAN BUSINESSWOMAN

WHAT? I really believe this last quote to be true in our sales world. This applies to service and products. For example, I was attending a big trade show recently to meet with some of my client organizations and the exhibit hall was flooded with a blur of salespeople. Everyone and everything started to look the same. In today's environment, the salesperson must create a unique customer experience in order to set himself or herself apart.

SO WHAT? If you are trying to convert a competitive account, but you look like and sell like your competition, then with all things being equal, why would the buyer change? If you attend enough trade meetings and go to breakout sessions, you will even hear your customers remark that they are bombarded with sales reps knocking on their doors and all seemingly saying the same thing.

As sales professionals, we are an extension of a direct marketing tool. Whether we want to admit it or not, we are an interruption to our customers. This interruption may be considered good or bad, but an interruption nevertheless. Therefore the need to separate yourself from your competition is more important than ever. I'm not saying you should go out and wear clothes that are not appropriate to look different and act in a manner contrary to your professional code. I am saying you are responsible for creating a brand image complementing your company, but that is also unique to yourself.

Consider this: The number-one thing that will keep you marketable are your customer relationships (past, present, and future). Those relationships are sacred ground and have a lifetime value. Research shows that the salesperson who acquires a customer will retain the customer (if you lose a customer, it will cost you 10% more to recover him or her). Consider all the lifetime revenue opportunities associated with creating a unique customer experience that captures and retains that customer:

- Residual revenue – baseline revenue that you can count on every year to help you achieve quota

- Solution expansion or increased wallet-share revenue – dollars generated from selling additional solutions to a customer

- Upgrade revenue – revenue derived from future upgrades (many software companies experience this type of revenue)

- Referral revenue – word-of-mouth advertising both internally to other divisions as well as to other organizations.

So, the more that you create an ongoing unique experience for your customers, the more you are increasing "career security."

As a new medical-device sales representative, I had firsthand experience with needing to separate myself from the competition. There was a competitive hospital that used only 10% of my products. I couldn't get access to the doctors or to the staff. So, one day I convinced the director of surgery that I needed to in-service (technical presentation) her staff on one of our products. Knowing that this was my one shot to build relationships, I bought fortune cookies the night before, broke them open, replaced the fortune with a customized fortune specific to that hospital and staff. During my technical presentation, I used the nurses' first names and when they got a question right, they won a fortune cookie. The fortune cookies said, "Dr. Smith will be nice to you today." Of course, the nurses thought this was hysterical because Dr. Smith was never nice to anyone. A few weeks later, when I was in the hospital to drop something off, a nurse came up to me and said, "Hey, fortune cookie guy, I've been telling the doctors that your technology has more safety mechanisms and Dr. Hampton wants to see you." Within four months, I had converted the entire hospital. How did that happen? Not because I knew my technical information, but because the nurses appreciated that I had spent the extra time to give them a unique edutainment experience (because I had shown that I cared, they were willing to share).

NOW WHAT? Consider everyday mundane business interaction and spend some time thinking about how to do it differently in order to separate yourself from the competition and drive customer rapport (edutainment). Here is the great news, it will end up creating a mutually enjoyable experience.

- The basics. Common sense but not common practice. The simple stuff that has survived through the ages because it works: warm smile; solid handshake; and sincere words of encouragement.

- Use people's first names. Remember their names and use them appropriately throughout the conversation.

- In general, get them talking about themselves. When appropriate, ask them about their family. How long have they been with the company? In their role? Where did they go to college? Where did they grow up? Careful, be sure that the timing of these conversations is appropriate to their personality. Some personalities don't want you to start the conversation with a lot of these questions. For some, it may only be appropriate to collect one friendly fact at a time.

- If a supervisor, talk positively about the staff. Notice little things about the staff ("Bob looks great, he lost some weight!!").

- Sincere and specific compliments. Your buyer will be more willing to share (and you'll get the important answers you need in order to shape your solution).

- Under-commit and over-deliver. Give 'em more than they asked for, but the key is to do it at the right time. Train yourself to save and then give extras after they have bought from you. Here are areas to provide additional commitments or service:

  - Beat expected delivery dates.

  - Provide more training than originally agreed upon.

  - Cost – at the last minute, provide a free product or a slightly higher discount (not much). They will trust you in all future dealings and give you future business opportunities.

  - Enlarge service agreement.

  - Extend warranty.

  - Any other extras????

- Ask them: "What will it take to provide you with the best service that you have ever received?" (The answers may surprise you: One customer responded that a salesperson shouldn't wear cologne because she is allergic; another said to be sure not to leave phone messages on Mondays because he is jammed; etc.).

- In his book <u>Loyalty-Based Selling</u>, Tim Smith notes that these are the core components of customer-friendly facts that you should know in order to build a strong relationship: full name; birthday; previous work experience; interests; spouse name/birthday/interests; high school (graduation date); college (graduation date and degree); hometown; religion. I also think Harvey Mackay's 66 is a good benchmark for what information to collect that will help retain that customer.

- Once you have these data, use a CRM (customer relationship management) software system (e.g. www.exsellerator.com) to notify you of these key dates and then send out cards.

- If you are sincere and feel so inspired, participate in one of their charities.

- And, one of my favorites is "planned random acts of kindness." I used to start the week off by finding gaps in my schedule and then filling those time gaps by stopping by customers just to say "hello" or drop off doughnuts. It trains the customers to realize that I'm not selling them something every time I see them.

- If you're involved in a business that needs repeat sales from all customers: The first time you meet buyers, don't sell them anything … this will insure that they will want to see you the next time.

- Appropriate humor. One of my first managers, Ed Traurig, was a master at keeping things light and fun. He has a rare genius at making people feel good. Besides being one of my first managers, he was one of the best.

- On the day of your sales call, if people are really jammed, say, "I can tell that you're really jammed, would it be better if I came back another time?" If the appointment does get rescheduled, they will be emotionally engaged and wanting to help you. You will get more accomplished in that meeting then you ever imagined.

43. SÉANCE SELLING: THE CLAIRVOYANT CONSULTANT

con·sul·tant (n.)
1. One who gives expert or professional advice.
2. One who consults another.

A consultant's main thought process must be ... how can I help contribute to my customer's profit?

MACK HANAN, AUTHOR OF <u>CONSULTATIVE SELLING</u>

A consultant is an experienced individual who is trained to ask questions, analyze, and provide a buyer with ideas that will help them make the best possible decision.

TAZ

sé·ance (n.)
1. A meeting of people to receive spiritualistic messages.
2. A meeting, session, or sitting, as of a learned or legislative body.

WHAT? This Illumination is not about how to be a sales consultant (Mack Hanan has done a phenomenal job explaining that in his Consultative Selling editions). This Illumination is how to be emotionally received as a consultant. The buyer has to believe that you are worthy of his or her time. You have to do that in a fashion that is nonthreatening and with a delivery that is likened to an empathetic servant. And, just as important, you can still be a professional when you deliver a spiritualistic, passionate message about increasing profitability.

SO WHAT? Buyers are more likely to believe that you are worthy of their time if you can quickly communicate your experience with helping other buyers who had the same issues. Also, you can ask more questions and get more real answers if they feel that you have the ability to help them. And, finally, they need to sense that you can help them avoid making errors (they have a fear of making the wrong decision).

NOW WHAT?

- Quote industry statistics. A consultant knows his or her buyers' industries and uses statistics (e.g. the average risk management expenditure is $31,300; the average small business spends 30% of its revenues on marketing).

- Evoke the "spirits" of other customer's experiences. Your buyers want to know that they are not alone. They want to know that you have helped other buyers who experienced a similar challenge. Nothing seems safer than not being the first, second or third person to try your solution.

- Your delivery of evoking the spirits should feel as if you have removed yourself from the room (metaphorically). Facilitate the conversation between the buyer and your current customers (e.g. if John were here, he'd probably say that he wished he had put more of his budget into our XY solution rather than into our AB solution). To do this more effectively, review the Illumination "Why Do Customers Buy?" and use that as a template of things to have the spirits focus on when they have a conversation with your buyer.

- Example: "My last seven customers have experienced similar challenges: They wanted to achieve profitability without reducing the workforce. They didn't want to see coworkers laid off. At the same time, they didn't want to risk making a bad decision that could affect their career." Notice the emphasis on EBM (emotional buying motives). Other examples of ways to start the conversation: "Many customers have told me," "There are a lot of industry articles saying that … "

- After facilitating the "spirits of current customers," be sure that you end that first meeting by looking into the crystal ball and painting your solution as the way for the buyer to remove his or her current perception of loss or pain.

44. THE FOUR WAYS TO INCREASE CUSTOMER RETENTION

I hear and I forget. I see and I remember. I do and I understand.

CONFUCIUS

WHAT? Methodologies for increasing your buyer's memory of your value proposition.

SO WHAT? Have you ever left a sales call and asked yourself, "Did they really hear me? Did I just sound like a rambling idiot?" If you feel that way, it probably happened that way!!

You need your buyers to remember your key selling messages and, with that, they will stay motivated to move forward with your solution.

NOW WHAT? Here are four ways to make your information "stick":

- Create a powerful picture. Paint pictures of pain ("Cindy, have you ever experienced the paper jamming in the printer? And you start tugging on the paper and it still won't come loose? And then the paper rips and you have to open the contraption … .")

- Power messaging (the Power of Three). Combine your customers' needs and your benefit into one or two sentences, and then say that sentence at the beginning of the meeting, during the middle of the conversation (casually), and then at the end. It works like subliminal advertising and hypnosis. Example: "You mentioned that you are trying to reduce your expenses by 11%, and my company is the industry leader at helping you achieve that objective by the end of the year."

- Professional coaching. Get them to repeat your key messages. Example: "We've talked about a lot today. I'm curious, what are the solutions that are most important to you?" If they miss a key one, you can add it in later by saying, "Yes, we can provide those solutions and also we are the least expensive when it comes to total cost of ownership."

- Engage all of their senses. Let them touch or work with your solution in some way, shape or fashion. The brain increases its memory if it engages and it actually will tactically feel the dimensions of something (if you sell something tangible).

45. GET KEY APPOINTMENTS

There are two levers for moving men: interest and fear.

NAPOLEON BONAPARTE

To gain people's attention, you must make them believe that they are missing out on something.

TAZ

WHAT? Master salespeople use a specific "attention-getting" science to gain access to decision-makers.

SO WHAT? How can you score a touchdown if you're not even in the game? Your buyers are busy. They don't have time to listen to every salesperson. You need to create a process for getting their attention.

NOW WHAT?

- Your objective is to create interest in 60 seconds or less.

- Tom Sawyer didn't beg the other kids to paint his fence; he got them to believe that they were the ones missing out on an opportunity. You must create the scenario in which the buyers feel like they are missing out on something.

- Go "high" fast. Find the highest-ranking person in the department or organization and reach out to him or her first. If you don't, you may get hung up with non-decision-makers who waste your time (and then, when you try to go above them, they get pissed and sabotage your efforts).

- Curiosity, fear, easy gain and pride get people's attention.

- Never, ever, ever use the following statements (kiss of death) in a 60-second pitch:

  □ Did I catch you at a bad time?

  □ How are you today?

  □ Is now a good time to talk?

  □ I'd like to learn a little more about your business to determine...

  □ I'd like to see if there are some ways we might work together.

- Here are the key components to help you create interest:

  □ Use your company name (if a top brand). Make a quick statement about your company (market share, money spent on R&D, the commitment that your company is making to innovation and or the buyer's industry). Too many reps miss the opportunity to say more about their company; they all want to jump into product features.

  □ Use the names of well-known customers (especially if you're not a brand leader).

  □ Credibility: the number of customers that your company has helped and the average performance metric that your solution provided ("We have worked with more than 300 customers in helping them reduce _____ by 24.3%.").

  □ Make blanket reference statements ("Many of our Fortune 500 customers have told us that efficiencies and bottom-line profitability are critical when they select _____ solution. Is this also true for you?").

- Gain references prior to making the call (which can be internal or external … internal sponsorship – a peer or boss). Try to never make a cold call!!! Cold calling is for losers.

- Use names of internal power players, a peer's or boss's name. ("I had a chance to speak with Jim Johnson yesterday and he noted that he was interested in trying to find ways to be more efficient to help drive the bottom line." By the way, this conversation did happen, but it was casually done at a social event or in the hallway. But the person with whom you are talking doesn't know in what context or environment that the conversation happened.)

- A very specific benefit statement (e.g. "We can help increase your margins by 13.9%") about your solution.

- Apply a time constraint or supply constraint. ("We only have the ability to add two more clients this year." "We are only able to deliver 11 more units in this calendar year.")

- Use a professional, enthusiastic and confident voice.

- Examples:

  - "Good morning, I'm Brad Smith with Infusion Technologies Galactica. Jim Johnson told me I should call you because we're the company that just helped [current customer] increase their profitability by 11%. Are you looking for solutions that can drive profitability? Good, because I still have room for five more installations this year and thought we could get together to see if we're the right solution for you." (This last statement has a "loss" element – they might lose out if they don't do business with you soon.)

  - "Good morning, I'm Brad Smith with Ultimate Galaxy Office Products. We're the company that just spent $5M on R&D in order to provide our current customers with an engineering project 'time reduction' average of 33%. Is your organization looking to get these kinds of results and increase your bottom line? Because we have a limited supply of technology trainers, we are only going to install our new solution into current customers first. However, we're in the process of identifying other organizations that may have interest."

▫ "Good afternoon. This is Brad Smith with Galactic Solutions. We're the company that has been helping companies like yours minimize their expenses and maximize monthly sales revenue. We just helped WXYZ decrease expenses by 19% and increase sales by 11%. I'm calling to see if you're satisfied with your current expenditures and sales performance."

▫ "Good morning, I'm Brad Smith with Ultimate Medical. I just met Dr. David Johnson at a conference in Miami, and didn't you two go through residency together? He was looking at our new solution for patient healing and said I should give you a call because he thought you'd be interested. In working with more than 1,000 cardiologists worldwide, we discovered that there are three major disadvantages to current patient healing technologies: 1)xxxxx, 2) Xxxxxxxx 3)xxxxxx . Are you also experiencing some of these issues? I will be in town next Wednesday; do you have 23 minutes to look at this solution?"

- Create your own 60-second "attention-getting" statement by using some of the components noted above.

46. OPTIMISM AS YOUR FRIEND AND FOE

When people decide arbitrarily to be optimists, they may miscalculate when it comes to serious crises, evildoing, wars, personal conflicts, etc. If they decide arbitrarily to be pessimists, they will miss many opportunities for joy, fulfillment, hope, and faith.

DEEPAK CHOPRA, LIFE AFTER DEATH

Perhaps the question is not "Is the glass half empty or half full?"; perhaps the first question is "Does the glass have water in it?"

TAZ

"The optimist sees the rose and not its thorns; the pessimist stares at the thorns, oblivious of the rose."

KAHLIL GIBRAN (1883—1931)

LEBANESE WRITER AND PHILOSOPHER

WHAT? Top salespeople are optimistic, and at the same time hold themselves accountable to an objective reality. You can feel their quiet "can-do" energy and at the same time look into their eyes and see the wisdom that has been gained from pain (acquired from being too optimistic on previous opportunities). They are best described as optimistically pragmatic.

SO WHAT? In research that was done by psychologist Martin Seligman, it was shown that through his work with Metropolitan Life Insurance Company sales agents, sales agents who scored in the top half for optimism sold 37% more insurance over two years than those in the more pessimistic bottom half. Sales agents who scored in the top 10% of optimism sold 88% more than those ranked in the most pessimistic 10%.

NOW WHAT?

- Be optimistic … optimism pays – handsomely.

- Too much optimism can have a negative effect on closing sales opportunities. Are you suffering from "deal" loss? Congratulations!!! "Pain" plants a flag of reality in the fortress of an optimistic heart.

- The trick is to have enough optimism to overcome obstacles but not so much optimism that you are blinded by the reality of the situation. F. Scott Fitzgerald said, "The test of first-rate intelligence is the ability to hold two opposing thoughts in mind at the same time." Play devil's advocate with yourself on every deal.

- We need to be able to deploy active and objective discernment, by having the courage to ask the right questions and by measuring the buyers' actions (are they investing in you by doing things for you throughout the sales process?).

- In many companies, the managers have become the de facto discernment facilitators because they can maintain a more objective opinion. Ask your managers about their thoughts on your key deals.

- Read the next Illumination to become a seasoned deal pro and a professor of deal discernment.

47. THE NUMBER-ONE REASON WE LOSE DEALS

*The ability for me to see you is masked by
the amount of attention you give me.*

TAZ

*I love me, you love me, let's sit around and
bask in that mutual interest.*

TAZ

WHAT? The common denominator of lost opportunities is that salespeople misinterpret the difference between an internal coach and a champion. When I ask salespeople, "What is a champion?" they respond that it is someone who gives you insider information and will stand up and fight for your solution even when you're not there (including committee meetings). Unfortunately, their definition stops there. The reality is that they have just described a coach, not a champion.

SO WHAT? No opportunity has ever been closed without having an internal champion. Because the coach is helping the salesperson, he or she assumes that the coach is the champion and so will focus on that person. Such salespeople even tell their manager, their significant other, and friends that "this is a done deal." It is a complete surprise to them when they don't win the deal.

NOW WHAT?

- Understand the difference between a coach and a champion. A champion is someone who has credibility within his or her organization and will support your solution. It's that simple and that difficult.

- You can't make a champion. The champion has already established credibility before you were ever on the scene. You can, however, groom such a person to be YOUR champion.

- Find the champion by asking people within your buyer organization, "The last time a decision was made, who was involved? Who does everyone respect? Who else should I be speaking with?" If you ask seven people this question, you are looking for the same name at least three of the seven times.

48. THE DECISION-MAKING BRAIN

A picture may paint a thousand words; but a picture of pain paints a thousand dollar bills.

TAZ

WHAT? Scientists have proven that there are multiple brains in our body (and they are not all in the cranium cavity; a great book on this subject is Dr. Robert K. Cooper's The Other 90%). One of the brains is highly predisposed to initial first impressions and evoking emotional responses (flight or fight) as well as processing information with visual aids.

SO WHAT? Some of the brains are more easily influenced and therefore require your attention to how those brains process information. For instance, it has always been said that human beings make decisions emotionally and then rationalize that decision. It's true!!! And, the key elements of the emotional decision-making brain include "video, audio, smell and touch." The most powerful persuasive communicators in history have always used stories, verbal pictures and images as a way to quickly influence. For the sake of keeping it simple, consider that every sale needs to include emotional reasons to buy (emotional buying motives) and rational reasons to buy (rational buying motives). If you can't get buyers excited emotionally (e.g. the belief that they have "pain," the belief that they will miss out, or the belief that they could have a greater "reward"), then you will not advance the sale. Also, if you don't have a decent rational outline, you may not provide them with the rationalization that they need to convince other people. So, the first filter in decision-making is emotional buying motives (EBM), and these are customized to the individual (opportunity for promotion; opportunity to leave work on time, etc.), and the second filter of decision-making is the rational buying motives (e.g. efficiency, ROI; cost-containment; etc.).

NOW WHAT?

- Human beings process information visually. Understand that the brain is wired to remember your solution via stories, because of the thousands of years of campfire experiences (cellular memory), so be prepared to tell stories.

- Painting pictures is the easiest way to have information stick. Also, if you're selling a "state- of-the-art" solution, you may have to provide experiential learning by comparing your solution to something that the buyer is already familiar with, for example, "Have you ever gotten your tire stuck in the mud? Isn't that a hassle to have that wheel keep spinning? Your current software program is kind of like that spinning wheel. Whereas, our new technology has the ability to slow down and grip the surface in order to provide better traction."

49. Do You Want the Red Pill or Blue Pill of Reality?

There are no facts, only interpretations.

FRIEDRICH NIETZSCHE

Nothing exists except atoms and empty space; everything else is opinion.

DEMOCRITUS

The way we see the problem is the problem.

STEPHEN R. COVEY

Listening to both sides of a story will convince you that there is more to a story than both sides.

FRANK TYGER

There is an objective reality out there, but we view it through the spectacles of our beliefs, attitudes and values.

DAVID G. MYERS, SOCIAL PSYCHOLOGY

WHAT? There is no reality. Only the perception of reality, and that perception is solely based upon the person that is observing … so multiple observers will see differing realities. Princeton University is known for the "observer factor," which indicated that even at the subatomic level, particles will react exactly the way the observer "believes" they will react (even if observer A had an entirely opposite belief to observer B's ... which should further support the concept of "intentional living and designing your life"). Even more fascinating is that scientists believe that there are four million data points impacting a person every second. However, the brain can process only approximately 200,000 of those four million. Here is the catch: If we were standing right next to each other, my brain will likely pick out a different 200,000 to process versus your brain's processing of a different 200,000!!!! It's amazing that human beings can even begin to understand each other.

SO WHAT? A master salesperson has to uncover the buyers' perception of reality. By uncovering the buyers' reality (not the salesperson's transferring his or her own reality onto the buyers), the salesperson can start to merge his or her own reality to the buyers' perspective and can help the buyers achieve their objective.

NOW WHAT? Do yourself a favor: Throw a reality rope to your buyer. When the buyer catches it (because you built enough rapport to have him or her be open to catch the rope), then you start asking questions that allow you to pull yourself closer to understanding your buyer's perception, one hand-grip at a time (one question at a time). What questions help you bridge the gap of realities? See the next Illumination.

50. Great Questions to Ask (Bridging Perceptions of Reality)

Seek first to understand, then to be understood.

STEPHEN R. COVEY

Judge a man by his questions rather than by his answers.

VOLTAIRE

All big-time consultants know that their questions land the deal.

TAZ

WHAT? Master salespeople ask questions that uncover "pain," perception of pain, or perception of "loss." They do not ask questions about product features!!! That is soooo old school. The best questions are ones that will uncover emotional buying motives as well as rational buying motives. Those are also questions that are about the buyer's need for a solution for: strategic value/financial value; job-technical-clinical value; and personal value.

SO WHAT? Oftentimes, as salespeople, we are so busy educating our customers on features that we don't uncover what our customer need or want in our solution. When you engage in that line of questioning, you are just like any other freshman salesperson.

Your customers will know that you are a <u>consultant</u> by the questions you ask. When you ask good questions, they start believing that you can help them solve their problem.

NOW WHAT?

- Begin the first question as a statement, so that they know that you have done homework on their industry: "Many of my customers are noting that the industry average profit margin is 3% … are you finding this to be true?" While this is technically a closed probe, it works because the buyers appreciate the fact that you've done your homework and therefore are worthy of some answers (once they know you care, then they will share).

- For big-ticket items, I read their annual report and start the conversation with a sincere compliment that turns into a question (i.e. "Congratulations on achieving a 7% profit margin when the industry average is only 3%. Do you think you achieved those results because you invested in new technologies that made you more efficient? " If they say "yes," the follow-up probe is, "Well, I'm glad to hear that, because I'm prepared to share with you other ways you can achieve efficiencies.")

- The best salespeople always contemplate three powerful questions before they start a sales call. Review the Illumination "Why **Do** Customers Buy" for ideas on better questions.

- I have found that I can ask a customer very tough questions as long as I ask in a respectful manner and once he or she can see that I have done some homework. The best way to show respect is to start with "tell me about" or "help me understand" whenever the question lends itself to that opportunity. Here are some of my favorites:

- Help me understand your top three objectives this year.

- Tell me about the challenges to those objectives.

- Help me understand what happens if you don't achieve those objectives.

- What are your top three key business drivers for your company?

- Help me understand how your department's performance will be reviewed. What are the metrics of success? Who normally reviews the performance with you?

- If you could change _____, what would you change?

- Help me understand what you look for … .

- What is your plan for … ?

- The last time you made a purchase like this, did you receive the results that you wanted? If not, why?

- What would you change in the criteria or process this time?

- Tell me about a purchase you made that you are still pleased about. What was it and why are you still pleased?

- What has changed in your environment that has made you interested in looking into my solution? (You are looking for pain/fear/loss.)

- What do you need to hear, see or touch in order to gather all information necessary to make a decision?

- Help me understand how you will be able to determine if you want my solution or not.

- What will be the timeline and who will be the decision-makers?

- Can you tell me what you would like to happen next?

- And I always ask this before I leave: What question should I be asking that I am not asking?

- Eighty-two of the most important questions that you could ask!! Here are "framing questions" that help keep the conversation focused and allow both you and the buyer keep the picture of pain in a frame. We've developed a list of the 82 most powerful questions that master salespeople and negotiators ask their buyers. It is contained below and you can use it for the next exercise.

- **Exercise.** Circle the questions that you like. And for REAL fun, put a star next to the questions that drive toward emotional buying motives and then put the letters RBM next to the ones that drive toward rational buying motives. Watch out!! You are looking for questions that could be both ... those are the most powerful!!!!!

1. Help me understand what is your main *objective*? (They might answer: "keep my boss off my back" or "gain efficiencies").

2. What are your top three objectives for your practice, department or organization?

3. How do you *plan* to achieve that goal?

4. What are the obstacles that you face in achieving that goal?

5. How does this fit into your CEO's top three objectives for the next 12 months?

6. What is the *biggest problem* you currently face?

7. What *other* problems are you experiencing?

8. What are you doing *currently* to deal with this?

9. Tell me about your current level of service ... has it been below average, average or above average?

10. In your practice, what is the most important thing you look for when it comes to a sales rep?

11. When have you switched vendors in the past? Why did you switch? (If you have switched vendors in the past, tell me about the reasons for those changes).

12. What is your strategy for overcoming these challenges or achieving objectives in the *future*?

13. What *other ideas* do you have regarding the strategy for the future?

14. What do you like about your current solution?

15. What don't you like about your current solution?

16. If you could change anything about the products or solutions being offered in the markets, what would you change?

17. What were the initial technical, clinical, financial (operational) and business reasons for having that product in here?

18. What other departments are looking to make purchases? Which departments usually get what they want? Why? (A way of uncovering the nontraditional competitor.)

19. What role do others play in *creating* this situation?

20. Who else, *besides yourself*, will be involved in making the decision?

21. Who else is *affected*?

22. If you could have things any way you wanted, what would you *change*?

23. How will this *affect* the present situation?

24. What would *motivate* you to change?

25. Do you have a *preference*?

26. What has been your *experience*?

27. Is there *anything else* you'd like to see?

28. How much would it be *worth* to you to solve this problem?

29. What would it *cost*, ultimately, if
    things remained as they are?

30. What *alternatives* have you considered?

31. What benefit would you *personally* realize as a result?

32. How would *others* benefit?

33. How can I *help*?

34. Is there anything I've *overlooked*?

35. Are there any *questions* you'd like to ask?

36. On a scale of 1 to 10, how confident do you
    feel about doing business with us? *What
    would it take* to get that up to a 10?

37. Are you working against a particular *deadline*?

38. How *soon* would you like to start?

39. *When* would you like to take delivery?

40. What do you see as the *next* step?

41. When should we get together to discuss this *again*?

42. Is there *anything else* you'd like me to take care of?

43. If you don't make a decision, what are the ramifications
    for your company or for you personally?

44. Who in your organization was unhappy the last
    time this technology purchase was made? Why?

45. The last time this purchase was made, was there
    anyone who was disappointed in the *process*?

46. What companies (specific to your technology) have
    you worked with throughout your career? Why?

47. What do you like about the current
    relationship with your sales rep?

48. Tell me about any meetings that you've attended that
    further enhanced your industry product knowledge.

49. Help me understand how you feel about change.

50. Help me understand the impact of past changes on your people.

51. Who do you include in decisions to make major changes?

52. Help me understand a past system-wide change you made that has been well-accepted by your people? Why did it go well? Why didn't it go well?

53. Is there a budget for this purchase?

54. Has your department ever bought out-of-budget before? Why and what happened? (No? Why not?)

55. What is the process for getting this into your organization?

56. How did that other piece of capital equipment get in here?

57. What are the challenges you see in achieving those objectives?

58. What were the criteria for selecting your current solution?

59. What is the most important to you and your staff?

60. What does the ideal result look like for you?

61. After the sale, how will this solution impact your day-to-day?

62. If this solution were in here today, how would it impact you personally on a day-to-day basis?

63. How will this purchase impact your organization's business?

64. If the wrong choice is made, how will it impact your world?

65. Whom else do you think I should talk to?

66. Whom else will be involved in this decision?

67. In past decisions, who were the people involved in the decision? Going forward, who do you think should be involved in this decision?

68. What are the decision-making criteria for this acquisition?

69. What was the process last time you made a purchase like this?

70. What were some of the challenges for you and your organization during this decision-making process?

71. Why aren't you using us now?

72. How would you fix this process moving forward?

73. Last time, you didn't pick my company; how are the process or criteria going to be different this time?

74. From your chair, what's the most important thing about buying this solution?

75. After the sale, how will this impact your organization in general? What other departments will benefit?

76. If the wrong decision is made, how will that impact your job? How will that impact other departments?

77. What does the ideal result look like for you?

78. Is there anyone who is not supporting my solution on this deal? Why?

79. Who do you think is going to fill the new job opening of _____?

80. What recent projects/purchases were you involved in and how did they go? (This helps uncover the role that this person may or not play.)

51. THE THERAPIST IS IN (LISTENING SKILLS)

In conversations, do you listen or do you wait to talk?

UMA THURMAN'S CHARACTER IN THE MOVIE PULP FICTION

The more you listen to me, the more I find you fascinating.

TAZ (ON BEHALF OF MANKIND)

WHAT? In our work as a consulting firm, whenever we discuss listening skills, the majority of salespeople admit that they know that they are not very good at listening. When the topic comes up, they want to know a scientific process for increasing listening skills (and we provide this for you below).

SO WHAT? Ask any sales manager, and you will hear that he or she is surprised by how many times salespeople miss a buying sign or "pain statement" by a buyer. Poor listening is almost an epidemic. When we miss buying signals, we increase our workload, extend the sales cycle, and allow the competition to find a way into the sales cycle.

NOW WHAT? Follow these steps for increasing your listening skills:

1. Focus your attention on the person with whom you are speaking and forget about everything else. Especially forget about your "to do" list. This is the step that most people never completely master. And, if you miss this step, the rest of these steps don't matter. I personally envision a

chalkboard with my "to do" list and I wipe away the list with an eraser so that this person has all my attention.

2. "Feel" the person's answer (you are being passively empathetic). Does his or her body language put an extra emphasis on something or someone?

3. Engage physically in the conversation by, at the appropriate times, nodding your head, moving your hands (in acknowledgement or surprise), raising your eyebrows, and/or adjusting yourself in your chair. This trains your body to stay focused and it physically shows that you are listening.

4. At certain key times, repeat what the person says. This helps for the following reasons:

   a. It makes the speaker feel good (because he or she knows that you are listening).

   b. You will remember it, because your brain heard it out loud.

   c. It allows you to stall for time while you collect yourself and your answer to a question.

   d. It helps you clarify the information before you respond.

   e. And, sometimes the buyer starts selling himself or herself on your solution before you have delivered any demonstration of value (because you are there when the buyer starts articulating pain, he or she automatically starts inserting your solution into the dialogue).

5. Respond to the person's dialogue only after following the first four steps noted above.

6. Tip: Don't just use this for business. To get better at listening skills, you must practice using these skills 24/7.

7. Ultimately, you are following a highly effective listening skill process that is used by many therapists. So, think of yourself as a business therapist as you engage in these listening techniques.

52. THE GREAT SEPARATOR

Despair is most often the offspring of ill-preparedness.

DON WILLIAMS JR.

Dress me slowly, I am in a hurry.

NAPOLEON BONAPARTE, PREPARING FOR BATTLE

I have yet to be in a game where luck was involved. Well-prepared players make plays. I have yet to be in a game where the most-prepared team didn't win

URBAN MEYER

WHAT? The great separator of performance is planning. In particular, pre-call planning.

SO WHAT? In our work, with more than 11,000 salespeople, we haven't met a top-performing salesperson who didn't plan for each sales call.

NOW WHAT?

- Fill out the sheet below for a sales call that you have tomorrow or this week. Do you see how much information that you are missing? Once you fill in this information, how much more confident are you?

- After you use the following template a few times, you can mentally run through the preparation stage by using the five W's of journalism (who, what, when, where and why) and then add "what if" and "what else." If you're with a manager, you should add "what's my role".

- Do a dry run out loud to practice the delivery of your key questions and messaging. Think of this as role-playing with yourself.

- In the future, invite a peer or coworker to join you on a call so that you can have a third party help you prepare and post-call calibrate (teammates, manager, product manager, etc.).

- The higher the price point of your product, the more preparation is required. GE Medical salespeople would spend two to three days prepping for a call that was worth $500,000+.

PRE-CALL PLANNING WORKSHEET

See next page.

How does this person make a decision? (Past purchase behavior–criteria and process)			
Where is the meeting?			
When?			
Why is it important to me?		Financial gain:	
Why does this person thing I'm meeting with him or her?			
Why will it be important to this person?			
How will I accomplish my goals?			
What materials will I need?			
What ifs?	Issue:	Answer:	
	Issue:	Answer:	
What else can I accomplish?			
Reasons to return (as well as "creating events" of trust):			
Friendly facts to collect (CRM:)			
Approach (starting the call); personality trait and reducing "call reluctance":			
Identify pain (three opening probes); uncovering EBM and RBM:	1. 2. 3.		

53. NINE STEPS TO A COMPETITIVE CONVERSION

"The future will depend on what we do in the present."

MAHATMA GANDHI (1869–1948)

INDIAN ACTIVIST

"Shallow men believe in luck, believe in circumstances...
Strong men believe in cause and effect."

RALPH WALDO EMERSON (1803–1882)

AMERICAN WRITER, ACTIVIST

Obstacles cannot bend me. Every obstacle yields to effort.

LEONARDO DA VINCI (1452–1519), ITALIAN

PAINTER, SCULPTOR AND INVENTOR

Man is not the creature of circumstances, circumstances
are the creatures of men. We are free agents,
and man is more powerful than matter."

BENJAMIN DISRAELI (1804–1881)

BRITISH PRIME MINISTER AND NOVELIST

WHAT? Competitive conversions contain similar elements of success. Previously we discussed PAIDA™ as a way to increase your skills by preparing, playing, reviewing, and then improving against a sales call process.

SO WHAT? If you knew what these elements were, you could break them down and master them for every competitive account scenario and therefore convert more accounts.

NOW WHAT?

- Here are the nine steps that are similar to every competitive conversion. There are at least two to five subcomponents (under each step) that should be customized for your environment.

    Level 1: IDENTIFY THE RIGHT ACCOUNT Pick current customers who are not buying everything from you before you pick competitive accounts.

    Level 2: PICK A PLAYER

    Level 3: LIKE YOU AND TRUST YOU Get one person from the buyer organization to like you and trust you by using the techniques noted in this book.

    Level 4: SELLING "CHANGE" Remove the person's perception of "change" by focusing on similarities of his or her current product features and processes while focusing on the benefits of your unique selling features. Your solution benefits must outweigh the emotional and rational cost of change (see the Illumination "Your Real Competition").

Level 5: UNCOVERING EBM AND RBM as they relate to all key players (EBM = emotional buying motives; RBM = rational buying motives).

Level 6: EXPAND (INTERNAL REFERRALS) And break down all the players using an analytical worksheet (www.warriorsalesmonk.com) and then look under the Matrix Complex Selling tab). Find all remaining players; start to identify and groom a champion.

Level 7: IDENTIFY DECISION-MAKING CRITERIA AND PROCESS Gain visibility to this information.

Level 8: IDENTIFY POLITICS Gain visibility to unofficial decision-making. The definition of politics is "allocation of limited resources." Is there someone who is telling everyone "it is my turn to get corporate funding … you'll have to wait to buy your solution until next year"?

Level 9: INFORMATION "GAPS" AND MARSHAL RESOURCES See the probability calculator in the Illumination titled "Is Your Deal Real?"

- What types of activities do I engage in throughout all nine levels?
  1. Rapport Building (i.e. Dominant Personality Trait and Trust Treats) and Trojan Horse
  2. Activities to uncover missing information (past purchase behaviors, perception of current pain, perception of solution for pain removal [desired state], key players/influencers)
  3. Activities to reduce perception of "change"

4. Activities that highlight value of your "pain removal" solution

5. Activities to leverage strengths (clinical, financial, strategic)

6. Emphasis on determining decision-making and purchasing process

7. Emphasis on understanding politics (unofficial decision-making)

8. Activities to disable competition (change; nontraditional; traditional)

9. Emphasis on finding champion

10. Activities to downplay weaknesses

11. Activities to groom my champion

54. DEADLINES ON THE CUSTOMER

The best defense is a good offense.

ANONYMOUS

Nothing feels better than a velvet hammer.

TAZ

WHAT? Buyers make purchases only when they perceive that the purchase will help them fulfill a need or a want. Research shows that human beings are more motivated and are willing to pay more for something if that something reduces their perception of "an impending loss" (compared to "reward"). In other words, the buyers must be feeling pain and their need or want is to relieve pain!!! The perception of pain or loss will motivate them into action. The classic example of this is when salespeople present the old supply/demand scenario by saying, "We have 123 customers who want this, but we only have 53 available to ship." The perception of losing out on an opportunity drives them into action.

SO WHAT? Decision-makers like making decisions. But, nobody likes to feel like they are being sold. SO, put them into the decision-making mode by giving them a narrow list of options (and many of those options have "pain" associated if they don't act now!!) from which they can choose (one of those options is "don't buy," and make sure that you can articulate the pain of staying status quo).

Give your buyers options that make them feel like they need to take action. Sometimes buyers are not aware of the whole pain/loss status of their own environment. However, if they don't perceive pain, we must create it so they can see the pain. If we do this, we will help advance the sale, get higher margins, create a potential referral, and establish a loyal customer.

NOW WHAT?

- Find out "why now?" There is always a precipitating event or factor that prompts buyers to be interested in your solution at this time compared with previous times. Why buy now? What happened in their business or personal life? What changed? Do you know why they couldn't or wouldn't buy last week, last month, last year? I have asked buyers this question, "What has changed that has you considering my solution?" What are they concerned is going to happen? (Was there an incident? A new problem? A mandate? Are they tired of coworkers nagging them? Is their boss on their back?) Do you know what benefit the customers will get if they buy now (i.e. recognition, achievement of another bigger goal, personal gratification, boss off their back, coworker respect? etc.)? Knowing the answer to that question can be a significant way to understand a customer and relate to him/her in a way that helps solve something that is very important to the buyer. More important, by your continuing to focus on that pain, it will keep them motivated to act (the sooner you implement my solution, the sooner you will realize the ROI that you wanted ... the sooner that you'll be able to present your boss with better results, etc.). Create a pain-relief time line in order to compress the sale.

- What would happen if the customer waited a week, month, year? Would he or she still accomplish the goal? Ask, "If you don't alleviate this pain, what happens?" Listen carefully to the response.

- If it's not clear to you "why they're interested in buying," you may have to create a hypothesis by asking yourself, "What prompted my last 10 customers to buy?" What was the pain or fear of loss that motivated them? Now, use those stories as examples of pain/loss for the future buyers whom you are going to be calling on in order to stimulate pain/loss conversations and have the buyers create a compressed time line to acquire your solution.

- Who else in the organization will be pleased by the purchase (other than your immediate contact)?

- Examples of "pain/sense of loss" deadlines to put on the buyer (you may wish to circle the ones that are relevant to your industry):

  □ Product scarcity (supply and demand).

  □ Future increase in pricing.

  □ Short-term pricing incentives that will go away.

  □ Product or solution lead time (the amount of time that it will take your organization to provide the solution … such as a manufacturing time line … so the buyer should buy today or the lead time will be extended).

  □ Training. If your solution requires some training component, discuss the limited amount of space in your training programs and the collapsing training calendar (not very many more training dates left).

- Impending industry or government reviews of their business that require the buyer to change something (OSHA, etc.).

- Your buyer's organizational growth issues (new building needs HVAC right now).

- The sooner the solution is installed, the sooner your buyer will see a ROI.

- Freight will increase.

- Beat the competition by being the first to have this solution.

- Construction deadlines.

- Interdepartmental battle for funds (if your buyer's department doesn't buy now, it may lose the funds).

- Press release time lines.

- Buyer's department has personnel who will be taking vacation (e.g. summer or holidays) soon and will not get full benefit of installation training and proper utilization.

- Finance scarcity and deadlines.

- Pole position for product launch.

- Risk management issues/edicts.

55. TELL 'EM, DON'T SELL 'EM

Fundamentally, customers don't want choice. They just want exactly what they want. Your job is to help them figure out what it is they want, because often they don't know or can't articulate it.

B. JOSEPH PINE, FAST COMPANY

Tell 'em, don't sell 'em.

STEVE O'BORSKY

WHAT? Help your customers set buying-criteria confusion, delusion and exclusion.

Our customers are confused. All products seem to look or sound alike. The days of a sales representative placing a product on a table and then spouting features and benefits have come to an end. The wise sales rep creates a criteria template — a formal or informal document that outlines the business or technical criteria that a solution should provide. Note: This is not a feature/function/benefit marketing slick.

The criteria template is presented to the buyer at the right time during the sales call. Completing this step is critical if you're selling a complex, constantly evolving or technical solution.

SO WHAT? Have you ever felt good after cleaning up your closet, your office or your car? That's exactly the way your customers will feel when you help them organize their thoughts. Life is so complex today that people are looking for things to be more simple.

By providing a criteria template, you are creating the opportunity to engage your clients in open dialogue. They would like you to help them narrow their list of needs and start including their wants (as if they were needs!). This is important because people will generally pay more for your solution if you help them achieve a want or emotional buying motive.

By getting your customers engaged in the process of more clearly articulating their criteria, they will become emotionally beholden to you. This works because you've helped them:

- Crystallize their thinking (and you were there when it happened, so they feel a connection with you).

- Clear up confusion (so they feel good).

- Realize that some of their needs can't be met in today's market (they were delusional).

- Understand that they may not need everything (exclude unnecessary features).

Ultimately, identifying the areas of need and focusing on their wants, excluding random, unnecessary or unrealistic needs, is a huge service to your customers.

NOW WHAT?

- It took me many years to learn the importance of "scripting" for my customers. Scripting is how to articulate for themselves and others involved in the decision process why this purchase decision makes sense. It's important to assist your customers in preparing responses to likely questions from other players inside their organization. Your job is to identify the common denominator needs from all players involved and help the key players articulate these. As you go through the criteria template, be sure to tell them why others have made similar decisions. This allows them to feel comfortable with the purchasing decision and helps you separate yourself from the competition.

- Review the reasons your last seven customers bought from you. Consider these key areas of your solution. Did it:

  □ Help drive strategic initiatives (including 12-month business objectives)?

  □ Make someone's job easier?

  □ Help the customer either financially or operationally?

  □ Achieve a personal win?

  □ Create a criteria checklist for your customers. Include information about the product as well as the reasons clients bought from you in the past. Expand the criteria to include your unique selling features. A checklist should include things like:

  □ **Strategic criteria:** The solution must provide a tangible plan to help the customer's organization drive market share (i.e. insert the organization's key business drivers or business objectives from their annual report). You may end up listing one to three criteria under this one. Other examples: profit margins, consumer awareness, shareholder value, market penetration, ease of global expansion.

  □ **Financial/operational criteria:** Show how the solution drives efficiency; removes redundancy; reduces employee overtime; increases cash flow. Include whether or not the solution is an "open platform or architecture" for future growth or integration of other solutions.

- □ **Job/technical criteria**: The end user criteria – this will be your biggest criteria area. It may start to look like a specifications sheet: Is it easy to use? Does it have a bright screen? What is the resolution of the screen? Does it increase visibility (of what the end user is working on)? Is it ergonomic? Is it reliable? Does it take up less space (footprint)? Does it require less manual effort? What is the PSI (pounds per square inch)? Does it integrate into other work-flow areas?

- □ **Personal value** (emotional buying motive or EBM): This part of the criteria should be delivered verbally. Address emotional questions such as: Will this allow the ability for the buyer to go home earlier? Get promoted? Satisfy staff? Stop complaints from other departments? Make a safe decision? Make a bold decision?

- It's critical that you consider the timing during the sales cycle to provide this criteria checklist. Some salespeople submit this early so the customer can use it as a "request for proposal" sent out to other vendors. Remember, if you help create the criteria, and it includes your proprietary features, you most likely will win the deal.

56. CONSULTANTIZER OR WIDGETIZER?

How do I impact my buyers' bottom line?

CONSULTANT'S THOUGHT PROCESS

How do I sell them as much of this product as I can?

WIDGETIZER THOUGHT PROCESS

WHAT? Companies that sell technical equipment (enterprise-wide computer sales, software sales, technical medical products) dedicate a technical expert and a salesperson to every sale. The salesperson creates the interest, determines the business need (not the technical need), and facilitates the dialogue between his resources and his buyers' needs (the technical person is always on stand-by during most sales calls to be prepared to answer specific technical questions that may arise). This is a winning formula, because the salesperson, in this environment, is so heavily focused on "How does my solution impact their bottom line?"

SO WHAT? No matter what you sell, you need to take a lesson from these high-powered technical sales organizations and relieve yourself from the tyranny of product features and focus just on how you can impact your customer's bottom line. This thinking process moves you from being transactional-oriented to creating a lifelong customer.

For most of my career, I have seen or consulted for sales forces that delivered technical, engineered, or sophisticated technology-driven products and solutions. The most effective teams separate the technical function from the selling function (technical people traditionally make terrible salespeople). By doing this, they have been very successful because the arrangement allows the salesperson to be focused on the business needs of the buyer. My father, who was handsomely rewarded for selling computers for Sun Microsystems (and was runner-up to being rookie of the year at age 54), has a BS degree in conservation and for the most part just barely knew how to turn a computer on.

When I started in sales, the classic sales approach was feature-benefit selling (nobody buys features, they buy benefits). Once I learned that, the rest of my training was all about the technical aspects of the product – the features. The rationale was that benefits are derived from the function of the feature. So then I was told it was really feature-function-benefit. Sales training has been evolving, and we have gone through needs-satisfaction selling, value-added selling, and now of course we are all selling solutions. However, all too often we talk about the great solution we delivered to the customer and then describe it by listing the bill of materials or the items we invoiced as the solution. I think we are still missing the boat. Or perhaps we are trying to get on the boat, but our customer is at the airport.

A real advantage for a nontechnical person selling technical and engineered products is that his or her focus has always been on what the customer wants to happen if they purchase from me. In selling technical products, most salespeople cannot totally explain the intricacies of how their product works, but they can talk about what their customer wants as *a result* of using the product/solution.

THE REAL WORLD From Gary Summy (former global director of performance development: sales and marketing, Motorola University): "Sometimes I would be asked for technical explanations and I would package them in terms of results as well as coordinate a call with my technical person. For example, I was often asked how a sophisticated AC motor-control panel worked. My standard response was that if you turned the knob on the right clockwise, the motor went faster, and counter clockwise, it went slower. You might be amazed at how often my answer was all they needed, especially if I would get the customer's engineers the documentation they wanted. Another frequent response was that while I was not an engineer, I had their phone numbers and I would get the information.

"The new buzz phrase is to sell solutions, but everyone is selling solutions. We need to go beyond solutions and focus on how you impact your customer's business. How are you valuable to their business? I worked for an executive in the mid-1970s that I think was way ahead of his time. He told me that the true value you bring is your ability to make your customer more profitable and successful. Solution-oriented selling is often focused on solving a problem or issue (I think that's where the phrase 'solution' comes from, I could be wrong), but customer value is all about improving your customer's business in a way that will position how you are valuable to their operations. How, where and to what extent you deliver that value determines how valuable you will be.

"You are valuable because you are part of the customer's success. It reminds me of when I was recruiting electrical engineers to sell electric motors and drives to industrial customers. We put on the University sign-up sheet that we were looking for EE or ME graduates. One woman on my schedule (circa 1980) was a chemical engineer. During the interview I questioned her degree, since we wanted the EE or ME graduate and asked how she saw her background fitting with our company. I still remember her answer. 'I understand process, and you sell to process industries. I know what your customers do and how they do it. I would expect you to help me understand how I can help them improve their operations.' I wish I could have hired her on the spot. Unfortunately, some more-glamorous companies saw the same talent I did and we never got a chance to hire her. It was our loss.

"Because I was not a technical expert, I had to identify how I could deliver value when it was traditionally defined as engineering expertise. I became valuable because I would focus on what the customer was trying to achieve, not how we made things work. In a way, it goes back to what I learned in feature-benefit selling. It is never about how it works, it is always about what it does for the customer. We have added scope to that benefit concept, where sales professionals are now looking at what it does through the customer's eyes and applying their metrics to measure value."

NOW WHAT?

- Remember, it is not, and probably never was, about what you are selling. It is always about what it does or delivers to the customer, whether it is a tangible product or a service-based offering. Much of the sales training you may have received is focused on how to position your product, how to identify the customer's problems and/or pain and how you can solve that pain. When you find yourself "pitching" your product, or following a questioning path that will help you frame how wonderful your product or service is, step back and walk around to the other side of the desk. Remember, the customer engages consultants (salespeople) and defines them as valuable because:
  - They understand my business, my markets and my challenges at a macro or 50,000-foot level.

- They can translate that understanding of my business, my markets, my challenges to my immediate business at the corporate and even department level.

- They focus on my metrics, my language and my issues with a genuine interest in helping my business succeed.

- If focused on a specific problem or pain I have, any solutions offered are defined in my terms and not described as a bill of materials or product set I need to buy.

- The salesperson creates the interest, determines the business need (not the technical need), and facilitates the dialogue between his resources and his buyer's needs (the technical person is always on stand-by, during most sales calls, to be prepared to answer specific technical questions that may arise).

- Ask yourself – how are you valuable to your full picture of the buyer's organization's profitability?

57. OVERCOMING OBJECTIONS

The word "no" to a master salesperson is similar to the sound of the starter gun during a sporting event.

TAZ

WHAT? Great salespeople reach a point in their careers in which they love to hear the word "no" when they ask a buyer to advance the sale. Many times, the word "no" is the sign that the real selling is about to begin.

SO WHAT? The word "no" could be the best word you hear in a sale! Why? Because the word "no" is still an emotional response. The emotion behind "yes" and "no" is like love and hate (at least there is emotion involved, which means the person is engaged). Truly, the worst thing you can hear is indifference (which doesn't make much noise) or the word "maybe."

Unfortunately, most salespeople don't know how to take the "no" emotion and convert it to a "yes." You have been conditioned to *not* like the word "no." We didn't like it as kids and we don't like it as adults!!!! This is a shame because when buyers say "no," it is highly likely that there will never be a time when they are more ready to say "yes" than right now!!! Never again will they be this interested!!!

Why don't more salespeople convert the "no" to a "yes"? Think about it – in your mind, when they voice an objection you truly believe that they are saying "no" to you, even though they are saying really saying "no" to something else!! And this causes your brain to freeze up. It locks up their brain via the emotional brainstem. Remember back to the last time that you heard the word "no," how did **you** feel at the exact time? Maybe you felt annoyed, frustrated, curious, anxious, angry (with yourself or your customer), disillusioned, or you could have been thinking, "Why is it that I always get the awkward customers?" It is highly likely that you will feel a mixture of all of these emotions (and not only that, you know very well that everyone has difficult customers!). And, unfortunately, as you are trying to deal with these unfounded emotions, you are losing your buyer's attention ... which only magnifies the situation.

One thing is certain, if you hear an objection from a customer you know that he or she **has** been listening to you and is interested enough to effectively question you about it – which means you are doing your job right! *Objections are clues to the buyer's thoughts.* Sometimes, however, the objection is stimulated because of misinterpretation of your conversation.

For example, I was involved in a sales call with the executive team of a company, and we reached the point in the conversation in which the CEO said that they weren't prepared to move forward. I asked his concern, and he said that our installation process was going to take too long. I apologized to him by saying "John, I apologize if I have left you with that impression. Other customers initially felt that way, and what they found is that we were twice as fast as any other solution ... which means we will help you drive profitability faster than anyone else."

NOW WHAT? Your job now is to move that "no" from the customers' mindset to a "yes"! Impossible? **NO, IT IS NOT!**

- You gotta love the word "no" because it is an emotion and that means they are engaged!!!

- Understand that they are *not* saying "no" to you!!!!! What you need to do now is to relax and think about what they are saying to you or asking you.

- Objections appear logical but are almost always emotional. You need to continue probing to find the reason for their emotional hesitation (e.g. "I have some testimonials from clients just like you that can show you how we did help them reduce their expenses. Would you like to speak with them, or is there another concern?"). I like this one because it tests them to see if they will put the time into making those calls or if they will finally tell me the real objection

- A sincere objection means sincere interest (congratulations)!!!

- The more objections you get during a sales conversation, the more likely you are of succeeding! On the other hand, it may be that it is likely that you are being set up so that they can support the competitive solution!!! Either way, you've got to keep probing. And, if you start suspecting that they are truly comparing your solution for the purposes of supporting your competition, then before you answer their question, clarify by asking, "I'm curious, why is that important to you? Because most of our current customers are benefiting from our solution by getting a return on investment that is 25% greater than any of our competitor's solutions and they have never asked that question. So I want to be sure that I understand the question better in order to give you the appropriate answer." The intent is to get them to start questioning the competition that they were just covertly supporting.

- Why are they saying "no" to you? Well it could be any number of reasons such as:

- Interest in your product, but they need further clarification.

- A misunderstanding of something you have said. (Have you used too much jargon in your discussion that created a misunderstanding?)

- A desire for more information, or they just do not see they need your product. (Whose fault is that?)

- Some objections are generated because the buyer is looking for justification to upper management.

- You need to think carefully about your response. But first, seek clarification that you FULLY understand the issue and confirm this with the customer. Guess what? Now they are engaging in the process of trying to buy from you. Take your time to THINK, ANSWER and CONFIRM.

- You need to create "reflex" answers to the common objections that you will encounter, so that your emotional brainstem doesn't derail you and you lose the opportunity to convert them. Even though you have these answers memorized, don't jump into the answer – it will sound canned. Pause thoughtfully before giving the answer.

- Answer carefully, but as soon as you can. This helps create a sense of conviction. Sometimes, silence is good – the buyers feel you sincerely digesting their concerns. Use it to great effect!

- After you have given an objection some thought, you may need further clarification, so ask an open probe. "Why is that?" is a pretty well-used and successful question; try it because it works!

- After they give an objection, avoid using the word "BUT" at all costs. This starts a tennis match that you will only lose.

- Answering the objection. The best way to answer an objection is to bridge from their objection to your answer by respecting the dignity of their thought process. Have empathy. Try using this statement: "I can see how you'd come to that conclusion, other customers initially felt that way. What those customers found was … our solution has fewer failure rates." This works because you are removing you and your company from being the expert (your current customers are now the expert in response to the objection).

- "Contract" with them regarding their objection. The best way to ferret out a false objection (they just want you to go away) is to say to them, "If I am able to answer your concerns, would you be willing to move forward with an evaluation?" If they hesitate or say "no" again, you can ask them why. But at least you know where you stand!!! Answer the objection and confirm that you have dealt with the concern they had. Now the customer is agreeing with you and is saying "YES" in their mind! Now could be a great time to close! The best person that I ever saw do this is Tony Recupero, who made millions of dollars as a VP of sales.

- Price is not an objection!!! It is a lack of perceived value. You have not clearly articulated the full scope of the value of the solution.

- Answers to objections need not be brilliant. Many times the answer to the objection is keeping the conversation going.

- Practice on your spouse, partner or children – you may be surprised!

- If you do not receive any objections – check the order book because that customer probably says yes to everyone!

- Of course, the best way to handle an objection is to prevent them throughout the sales process!!!!

58. REDUCE THEIR RISK (OF SAYING "NO")

For buyers, it is easier to say "no" then to risk the unknown.

TAZ

WHAT? There are common concerns that every buyer communicates. Why not answer those concerns during the sales call rather than letting them try to assess those concerns on their own?

SO WHAT? When buyers have a concern, they get "locked up" and won't move forward. They become paralyzed in their decision-making because it seems that things are not clear. It extends your sales cycle and may cost you the deal.

NOW WHAT?

- Pretend that you're their boss. How would you review the buyers' decision to purchase your solution? Would you look just at the cost or would you also look at the return on investment? You must help the buyer prepare a document that lists the pros and cons of staying status quo and a second document that shows what will happen if they buy your solution. Then create a summary one-sheet review of the pros and cons of buying and not buying.

- "Risk" is a relative term that can only be defined by *their* personal outlook on life; so look at their past purchase behaviors and actions in their personal life to see what they consider to be "risky."

- Be prepared to present references, financial calculations, peer survey, and evaluations showing that subordinates are in favor.

- Identify their perception of risk (ask them, "What are the risks associated with this purchase?"). Remove their perception with facts and examples.

- Identify their perception of their current situation (pain/loss scale). "If you don't purchase my solution, what are the costs associated with staying status quo?"

- Offer a pilot project: "If you don't like it, don't buy it."

- You may have to uncover and then help remove these common concerns and roadblocks:

  - Lack of perceived **value** in the product or service.

  - Lack of perceived **urgency** in purchasing the offering.

  - Perception of inferiority to a **competitor** or in-house offering.

  - **Internal** political issue between parties/departments.

  - Lack of **funds** to purchase the offering.

  - **Personal** issue with the decision-maker(s).

  - **Already has a current initiative** with an external party.

  - "It's **safer** to do nothing" perception.

59. YOUR BEST DAY ... SCORECARD

Simplicity is the ultimate sophistication.

LEONARDO DA VINCI

The right activities, done right, lead to the right results.

TAZ

When you shift people's perceptions, their actions follow.

RAYONA SHARPNACK, FOUNDER, INSTITUTE

FOR WOMEN'S LEADERSHIP

WHAT? Haven't you finished a day in white-collar sales and asked yourself, "What did I do today?" I have always been jealous of construction workers because they leave every day being able to visually see what they have accomplished. The closest feeling that I have to that comes from mowing my lawn. I get to see where I started and how much more I have to go. Wouldn't that feel great if we could have that feeling every day or every week? The key is focus on the key activities, not the number, in order for you to be successful.

SO WHAT? If you follow a scorecard that focuses on achieving key activities, *you will be able to clearly see what you have done and it will make you feel successful every day ... even during a long sales cycle.*

Most salespeople work alone and then need to have feedback in order to know they are doing the right things. Why do you think new salespeople call their training brethren all the time? They do that in order to get confirmation of doing the job "right." What if you could develop a system that identified the key things to be doing and then how well were you achieving those things? You would compress the time it takes to hit your number!!!!

If you engage consistently in revenue-producing activities during the recognized work hours of your clients, you will place yourself in what I call a "revenue-producing posture." We are all responsible for delivering the sales number assigned, but can often lose sight and even hope if we don't have a way of evaluating whether we are successful on a daily basis. And, being successful on a daily basis allows us to be successful in the big picture.

Prior to knowing each other, Matthew Scott (cofounder of Strategic Incubator) and I had both independently established the need for creating daily scorecards in our separate organizations. Here is Matthew's story:

"I entered sales with a new start-up company, where each of us had zero business in an already competitive industry. I sold very little in my first three months and became discouraged. I fell into the trap of thinking if I just worked harder, traveled more … then I would be more successful.

"I applied an idea that was not original, but worked for me. I reasoned if I figured out specific, revenue-producing activities needed to engage on a daily, weekly and monthly basis, and if I did them consistently with the right attitude, that I would no longer question at end of day if I was successful. I sought the advice of the best of the best in my company and even outside of my company in completing my revenue-producing activities list. The list is as detailed or as general as you want.

"I applied a point total to each activity. The higher-relevance activity would earn a higher point total. My goal was to accumulate 25 points a day."

Here's an example of how you might put together a scorecard for yourself:

2 pts.	Gathered information about a decision-maker (from the buyers' staff, other companies, other influencers inside that account).
2 pts.	Made contact with a decision-maker.
2 pts.	Uncovered the decision-maker's needs and wants.
2 pts.	Demo of our solution.
3 pts.	Referral from decision-maker.
3 pts.	Attendance of buyer at a company-sponsored educational event.
4 pts.	Gained commitment from buyer to advance the sales process (the buyer sets up additional appointments and involves other people).
5 pts.	Received a yes or a no from a buyer concerning a sales proposal.
5 pts.	Made one more extra sales call that day.

NOW WHAT? Put together a "model day" and weekly scorecard that assigns point totals to each activity. Set a minimum score that you want to attain (e.g. 100-point week and 25-point day).

- Average number of outbound calls per [day, week, month] (method typically used – phone, in person, etc.) to engage in an initial sales interview.

- Average number of initial sales interviews or demonstrations per [day, week, month] to find a highly qualified prospect where a contract or proposal will be developed and delivered.

- Average number of contracts or proposals delivered per [day, week, month, quarter] to close a deal.

Even sales-support people can benefit from this. Here is an example of a sales-support scorecard.

Sales-Support Personnel Weekly Scorecard			
ASR Name:	Joe Support	Date:	This week
Event		Points	Qty
Write proposal for account		25	
Write financing proposal		40	
Research on internal sales operations data base to determine sales opportunities		25	
Research service contract for account		25	
Order literature		10	
Research organizations' financials		30	
Research individuals' buying history		20	
Network w/other reps		25	
Network w/other divisions		25	
ID a new sales opportunity		50	
Present to buyer not using products		50	
Ride along with tenured rep		30	
Spend time in personal development		10	
		Total of Events	0

60. RULES OF ENGAGEMENT :THE DANGER OF CUSTOMER RELATIONSHIPS

WHAT? Can a strong personal relationship with a customer actually hinder your ability to sell? Strangely, yes. This sales challenge is more common than you might think and is prevalent in business's where sales people have consistent contact with the same customers.

Many salespeople have struggled to get past this relational road block and many managers have been frustrated by the lack of true selling to these important customers (but many times they let their frustration subside because they convince themselves that "at least there is a good relationship").

SO WHAT? You see your customers often and if they have no idea when, where or how you might try selling to them it makes things a bit awkward. What many salespeople do to remedy this problem is stop selling altogether and rely solely on the relationship.....big mistake.

You could lose business because of 3 scenarios that can be precipitated by having a strong customer relationship:

1. Creating an opening for the competition. Over time relationships with customers can become strong and salespeople often begin to rely solely on their relationship but there is great risk in doing business this way. Ironically it is often easier for a less known competitor to sit down with your customer and

have a deep dive sales call and the customer starts feeling special because of all of the attention.

2. When a salesperson is routinely in an account the relationships typically become comfortable. Sometimes the salesperson becomes close personal friends with one or more key customers in the account. This can be good and bad. Good because the salesperson enjoys unfettered access to the customer and bad because close friends seldom say, "Hey pal can you sell your product to me so that I really understand why I use your latest stuff." In this circumstance the salesperson often sells less often or not at all and relies too heavily on the relationship to carry the day. This is a surprisingly fragile environment for the salesperson. Other key players in the account likely care about things like price, quality, and technology and may challenge your position. This is less likely to become a serious threat to your position if your key allies are armed to defend your turf. If however the best that they can come up with is he/she is a good guy/gal you could be in trouble.

3. One other common scenario is handling the promotion from an account service role to a sales role. This is a common career path in many industries and is fraught with roadblocks that usually go unaddressed. When a person is in a service role the relationship is "pure." What I mean by that is that the person has no ulterior motive, is paid relatively the same no matter what the account buys that month and in short has only an agenda to serve. When their title changes and "Service" person is replaced by "Sales" person a

change in perception can begin to happen. This change happens to some degree in the mind of the customer but often to a much larger degree in the mind of the salesperson. The salesperson now has motive, incentive and urgency. Their agenda is different and this new view of themselves can feel very awkward. The customer can sense a shift in approach and when left undefined it can cause even the best relationships to sputter.

NOW WHAT? Customers need to see you coming! You can turn the relationship to your favor but you must be very deliberate and transparent in that process. Many salespeople try to perfect the art of weaving in and out of personal relationships and selling. I once heard the following statement when describing a salesperson that solely used relationships to drive their business, "They are such a great salesperson the customer didn't even know they were being sold." Hmmmm. I am not sure the customer would be thrilled to hear that comment and further the customer was almost certainly more aware than you suspect. It is this type of approach that lends to the image of the deceptive or insincere salesperson. It is vital that your customers see you coming. This is particularly true in situations of multiple sales or service contacts per month or when a salesperson moves from a support function to a sales function.

In general, consider making formal business reviews on a predictable basis (once a month, once a quarter, , twice year, etc.). These business reviews will help give you the opportunity to uncover new "needs" and at the same time remind the customer of your valuable solutions and service. Why does this work? Think about your best personal relationships. One thing that is likely true of these relationships is that they are somewhat predictable. Not predictable in a mundane or boring way but in a comfortable and reassuring way. There is a comfortable flow and reasonable predictability that allows a closeness and comfort level that good relationships share. Without the "predictability" characteristic relationships can fail to flourish.

In all 3 scenarios above, Rules of Engagement are very effective in moving the relationship forward on both a business and personal level. The broader relationship actually becomes less formal when the selling part of the relationship becomes more formal! When a customer knows what to expect and when to expect it the relationship can move forward more effectively. Your Selling time and Selling environment are two things that should be well defined in order for your relationship to flourish.

The Set Up of this new way of doing business is vital. The customer must first understand why a change in the way you sell to them is needed. These conversations can be surprisingly easy once the logic and imperative for doing so is fully understood. Examples of such set up conversations are listed below.

EXAMPLE NUMBER 1:

"Customers name to be of greatest service to you it is important that I constantly strive to understand your business, provide solutions, and do a thorough job helping you understand our solutions and how they can benefit you. I am in here so often that it is not necessary or practical for me to try and sell to you every time I come through the door. Even though I am here often I am not always able to take the time necessary to ensure your understanding of our product. Rather than hope that I catch you at just the right time when your have plenty of time to talk about your needs and our products it would be best to plan our time in advance. Your relationship is important to me and ensuring your thorough understanding of our products is as well. If we could formalize our selling time I think it would help. We will arrange it ahead of time and both know why we are there. Outside of those deliberate selling times I will be here for any other needs and to take great care of the account but selling will be reserved for that time. What do you think?"

Will there be opportunities to sell and reinforce your product or service at other times? Certainly there will be and you should take them! Formalizing the selling time leaves your customer better informed and builds walls around your account far stronger than those that are built with relationship alone.

EXAMPLE NUMBER 2:

"Customers name. In my new role I have sales responsibility and I have been thinking a great deal about how best to make this transition. If we could be clear about selling time it would allow me to firmly segment that part of my job so that I sell to you only when we are both prepared. I would like to make appointments to sell to you that are planned well ahead of time so that I do the best job I can helping you understand the benefits of our products while not changing the balance of our relationship."

61. RECHARGE YOUR COMPETITIVE ADVANTAGE

Identify, commercialize and renew your energy source.

TAZ

WHAT? You are your single greatest competitive advantage. What are you doing to maintain your energy, focus and edge?

SO WHAT? Have you had the experience of staring at a piece of paper or computer screen and re-reading the same thing over and over again? Meanwhile, minutes and hours slip by. On the other hand, have you had the experience of quickly finishing high-quality work? What was the difference? Most likely the difference is that your brain and energy had been allowed to rest prior to jumping into the work.

There is a famous dialogue that occurred between da Vinci and a bishop in which the bishop asked him, "Why are you not working on the painting that I commissioned?" While still lying in the field, da Vinci responded, "But I am working on it." He would defocus himself in order to recharge his energy and thus create some of the world's most famous art work and engineering designs.

When I step away from a project or an important sales call, I find relaxation in an activity such as running, tennis, reading, boating. When I come back to the project, I find that I have renewed energy and vitality and I actually complete the project sooner than expected.

NOW WHAT? Take some time to recharge yourself.

- Step away from a difficult project and take a break. (The break doesn't have to be "lying down in a field." It could be reading a book.)

- Energize your work life by having life outside work.

- Find a hobby that you love and use that to recharge your energy.

- Make sure that you are focusing on activities that impact your four performance batteries: spiritual, emotional, physical and mental. By making sure that you are effectively balancing the energy in your batteries, you will recharge your overall energy.

62. LIFE IS A GAME

Keep it loose or you create a noose.

TAZ

WHAT? Every game usually has the same components: basic directions; gray areas of the game (if it wasn't defined in the directions and it can improve your situation, gamers will take advantage of it); milestones to measure your status; a final review of the standings (winners, losers); and a deeper understanding that it is only a game (it shouldn't be taken too seriously and nobody should be getting hurt).

SO WHAT? Top performers love to view their daily, monthly, and annual efforts of selling as a game – complete with a system of ethics. All like to keep score. It keeps the day-to-day fun and challenging. By making it a game, it also keeps it light and loose (so they don't get tight and create a noose).

NOW WHAT? Think of your life as being a combination of Xbox and the movie Matrix. You're the main character in the movie and you're living in a computer simulation that allows you to shift realities as well as make advancements to other levels of the game. You need to be able to do this in order to survive and advance. While in this mode, understand that the computer simulation has been designed to throw the following things at you:

- Unexpected Adversities

- Time management

- Financial hardship

- Spurts of happiness

- Interpersonal conflict

- Other people's misconception of you

- Real and perceived challenges

Most important, understand that this has been a computer simulation. You can reset and start over without unplugging!

CONTRIBUTORS

MARY A. ELLIOTT BASSETT

Mary Elliott Bassett served as worldwide director, sales and customer training at Eastman Kodak Company for 12 years, managing the sales, marketing, and customer-training activities for the motion picture industry. In this role, Mary had worldwide responsibility for determining training needs, developing educational strategies, and implementing training programs to support Kodak's business goals and customer needs. Over the course of 29 years, Mary has held a variety of sales training positions supporting several organizations across all Kodak businesses.

PAUL BERGMANN

Paul brings an extensive background in research, software development, data analysis, data mining and decision support to FullView Solutions. As vice president and chief technology officer of New Standards, Inc., Paul actively led the development and application of intelligent technologies to analytic and decision-making challenges in the health-care and financial industries.Paul holds bachelor's and master's degrees from the University of Minnesota. A member of the Institute of Electrical and Electronics Engineers (IEEE), the American Computer Society (ACS), the Association for Computing (ACM), and the American Association for Artificial Intelligence (AAAI), he is an accomplished software developer with a strong foundation in mathematics and statistics.

An expert in the application of advanced measurement, psychometrics and machine-reasoning technologies to real-world problems, Paul has consulted and provided training in a number of industries, including health care, banking, target marketing, home mortgage servicing, and underground imaging. Specific companies include Stora

Enso North America, Andersen Consulting's Advanced Technologies Group, Object Products, Inc., LexisNexis, Mercantile Bancorporation, First National Bank of Omaha, Scudder, Stephens and Clark, Residential Funding Corporation, Credit Suisse First Boston, CentraCare HealthSystem, and Taylor Corporation.

JOHN E. DAVIS

John has spent 22 years in sales and sales leadership. He began his career with Novartis, serving as sales representative and district manager. In 1995, he moved to Medtronic's Cardiac Rhythm Management Division. While at Medtronic, he won the company's President's Club Award three times, as sales rep, district manager and vice president. In 2005, he won Medtronic's highest global honor, the Star of Excellence Award for his team's work in field force sizing and deployment. In 2008, he moved to St. Jude Medical as vice president of cardiology services. He has managed sales teams of more than 230 people and more than $275 million in annual revenue. John has presented his thoughts on sales leadership to various audiences, including sales management teams throughout the U.S. and in Asia. He holds a bachelors degree in English and lives in Atlanta with his wife, Melanie, and their two children, Elizabeth, age 12, and Walker, age 9.

NIGEL HIRCOCK

Starting his career as a sales representative in the pharmaceutical and medical device arenas, Nigel quickly gained a reputation for being a performance development architect. Currently, he is a director of global training and has successfully navigated the global development challenges as his organization has continued to drive double-digit growth inside a multibillion-dollar parent company. He has been responsible for the UK, then Europe, Middle East and Africa (EMEA) and now his responsibilities cross the globe and involve more than 400 representatives and more than 75 managers.

BILL JEWETT

Bill Jewett has been a successful sales representative, regional sales manager and sales training manager with a Fortune 500 medical device manufacturer. He has a master of business administration from Northeastern University and bachelor of science in economics from the United States Naval Academy. He is also a disabled combat veteran, attained the rank of lieutenant commander in the United States Navy SEAL Teams, and was awarded the Bronze Star for heroism in Operation Iraqi Freedom.

Bill has a Master of Business Administration, MBA from Northeastern University and Bachelor of Science BS in Economics from the United States Naval Academy. He is currently a business manager in the medical device and computer software market.

KATHLEEN M. LECK

Kathy Leck is a proven executive in management, business education, consulting and coaching, with more than 30 years' experience in a variety of industries. She has leadership expertise especially in major organizational change, mergers and acquisitions, performance consulting, and program and policy development. Since 1998, she has served as the executive vice president of the corporate education programs of Lake Forest Graduate School of Management (LFGSM). In that position Kathy is responsible for strategic direction, business development, administration and design and delivery of nondegree leadership learning solutions. LFGSM is an independent, not-for-profit business management education enterprise dedicated to improving the competence, confidence and ability of working professionals and organizations.

Since 2002, Kathy has served as an active mentor with Mentium 100, mentoring high-potential executive women. She is a sought-out public speaker and has presented on a number of leadership topics in the U.S., Europe and India. Kathy has a bachelor of arts degree from Northeastern University and a master of science from National College of Education; is a certified senior examiner of Quality and Performance Excellence, Illinois; and is a graduate of Corporate Coach University.

RENIE McCLAY

Renie McClay has managed training for three different Fortune 500 companies: Kraft, Gerber, and Pactiv. She trains audiences in person and via Webcast in North America and globally. She designs and delivers learning to improve performance.

Renie helps companies to improve creative thinking and innovation. She is certified in accelerated innovation and was trained in improvisation with Second City. She uses these tools help companies develop more productive and innovative teams. She has done work for retail, consumer products, packaging, technology, building products, information technology, hotel/hospitality, and health-care industries.

Renie is the past president of the Professional Society for Sales and Marketing Training (www.smt.org). She also directs the sales training forum for the Chicago Chapter of the American Society for Training and Development (www.ccastd.org). She is a judge for the American Business Awards.

She has authored *10 Steps to Successful Teams, Fortify Your Sales Force: Leading and Training a Strong Team, The Essential Guide to Training Global Audiences,* and *Sales Training Solutions.* Her company is Inspired Learning, and she can be reached at www.inspiredtolearn.net, 847-215-2364.

MATTHEW SCOTT

Matthew entered the U.S. Army in 1985, serving in various leadership positions as a psychological warfare specialist, commanding combat medics during Operation Desert Storm in Iraq, and as a paratrooper captain with the legendary 82nd Airborne Division. In 1994, he made the decision to leave the military and chose a position as a sales and marketing consultant in the biotechnology and medical-device market. Within seven years he was a co-developer and a vice president, sales, for a biotechnology company in San Diego, California. In 2004, the biotechnology business unit Matthew co-developed, sold for 16 times earnings. Matthew is a professional executive transition coach and works exclusively with executive and entrepreneurs in professional transition. Matthew's pragmatic real-world corporate and entrepreneurial success, combined with applying behavioral sciences (psychological warfare) in a unique learning environment, makes him a sought-after transition guide.

Matthew serves as the founder and managing director of The Strategic Incubator, a global strategic implementation firm equipping entrepreneurs to monetize and repurpose a business idea with a systematic revenue-producing virtual business development process into a time-shifted and on-demand product or service. As a chosen speaker for the prestigious Five Star Speakers, Matthew speaks to thousands of people every year on business development topics and creating strategic life-and-work design for entrepreneurs.

Matthew completed his master's degree in management in 1991 and completed certification as a Certified Professional Coach sanctioned by the International Coaching Federation (ICF) in 2006.

Matthew resides in Oregon with his wife and three children, living with intention next to the ski trails of Mt. Hood and the vineyards of Willamette Valley.

MARK SIMS

Mark has more than 24 years in sales and sales management; the past 22 of those years have been with a $6 billion Fortune 500 company. Mark is a regional sales manager for a capital equipment company and the director of the associate sales representative program for the United States. Mark is a guest lecture for the University Alabama Birmingham Med ID program and serves on the board for the program. He is a certified facilitator for the Matrix Achievement Group (a sales-force development consulting firm). A graduate of UAB in 1984, Mark lives in Birmingham with his wife, Jill, and their three children, Payton, Darby and Collin.

TIM SMITH

Tim Smith, the author of *Loyalty Based Selling*, became the number-one salesperson at his company at age 24, and has earned that distinction 10 times. He is currently a sales representative at a billion-dollar company, where he continues to set world records for annual sales. He lives in Grand Rapids, Michigan, with his wife and two children.

GARY SUMMY

Gary Summy has more than 30 years' experience in sales, sales management, and sales force development, providing value and insight to companies in manufacturing, distribution and services environments with significant emphasis on electronics, technology and communications. Gary is currently director of sales development for Trane Commercial Systems. Prior to joining Trane, Gary was global director of performance development for sales and marketing at Motorola, Inc. For the past 10 years he has been a leader in developing consistent processes for account and opportunity management across diverse global and product environments.

Gary was selected by Sales and Marketing Management magazine as "Sales Trainer of the Year" for 2002 as a part of its National Sales and Marketing Awards program. Although still primarily in a sales training role, Gary was a finalist for a "Stevie Award" as best sales manager in the 2004 American Business Awards. He is a member of the board of directors of the Strategic Account Management Association (SAMA) and president and a member of the board of directors for the Professional Society for Sales and Marketing Training. Gary lives and works out of his home in the Cleveland, Ohio, area, where he and his wife, Laurie, daughter Kyle, and son Greg enjoy active participation in the local community.

DIRK WAEDEKIN

Dirk Waedekin started his career in market development in the consumer products industry. One year later he was hired as a surgical sales consultant for United States Surgical Corporation. At USSC, Dirk consistently received recognition for outstanding sales performance including a national award for new product sales. In his 12 years with USSC, he was responsible for achieving performance objectives while functioning in the capacity of strategic leadership roles including: key hospital manager, regional sales director, divisional business director, as well as cardiovascular specialist. In 2001, he joined Kyphon, Inc. as a spine consultant and grew the Wisconsin territory from $150,000/year to more than $6 million/year today. He has won numerous awards at Kyphon, including President's Clubs and MVP. He is a national field trainer and maintains one of the top five territories in revenue at Kyphon and has a company record of 28 consecutive quarters attaining quota.

ABOUT THE AUTHOR

Todd Zaugg started his career in market development in the consumer products industry. One year later he was hired as a surgical sales consultant for United States Surgical Corporation. As USSC grew from $250 million to $1 billion, Todd consistently received recognition for outstanding sales performance. In his 10 years with USSC, he was responsible for achieving performance objectives while functioning in strategic leadership roles including director of managed care strategies, director of national contracts, and divisional business director.

Upon leaving medical-device sales, Todd became involved in the senior management team of three start-up companies (one was sold for $30M). Todd's background and experience provided him with the ability to quickly diagnose and effect the critical success factors related to business strategy, people and processes. He earned the reputation of successfully creating, developing and implementing the necessary business components for revenue growth in a compressed time frame. His key areas of experience include hiring, training, measuring and motivating high-performance teams and their leaders.

In 2001, Todd founded Matrix Achievement Group, LLC. Matrix is a global sales force performance-improvement firm whose mission is to help companies develop and sustain competitive advantage through consulting, training and coaching solutions. Matrix leverages the collaborative knowledge and experience of former sales executives, customer industry experts, and adult-learning professionals. The Matrix network has trained more than 11,000 salespeople and more than 973 sales managers in Fortune 500, Fortune 1000 and start-up companies. The

Matrix client portfolio reads like a "who's who" of the most revered sales forces in the world.

Today, Todd is recognized in the industry as a sales leader, a sales process engineer, and a highly sought-after keynote speaker and facilitator.

Todd lives in Memphis, Tenn., with his wife and their three children. He finds sanctuary looking over the cliffs of Pickwick Lake. His family is an active contributor to Habit for Humanity, Coaches Time Out, and Swing for the Cure.

TreeNeutral

CPSIA information can be obtained at www.ICGtesting.com
Printed in the USA
BVOW040843291111

277152BV00002B/47/P